Schoenberg's 'Moses and Aaron'

MOSES AND AARON, IN THE BERLIN PRODUCTION
OF THE OPERA, 1959

Schoenberg's
'Moses and Aaron'

KARL H. WÖRNER

Translated by
PAUL HAMBURGER

*With the complete Libretto
in German and English*

ST MARTIN'S PRESS
NEW YORK

Printed in Great Britain

Library of Congress Catalog Card Number 64–14229

© 1959 by Verlag Lambert Schneider, Heidelberg
English translation © 1963 by Faber and Faber Limited
Libretto © 1957 by Mrs Gertrud Schoenberg

Contents

Illustrations

Acknowledgments

(MUSIC EXAMPLES)

Examples 1–47 are reproduced by kind permission of B.
Schott's Söhne, Mainz; Examples 52 and 53 by kind permission of Universal Edition, Vienna; and Example 54 by kind permission of
Boelke-Bomart, Inc., Hillsdale, New York, U.S.A.

Publisher's Note

The English edition contains some important additions and revisions that were prompted by the author's impressions at the performances of *Moses and Aaron* in Berlin in October 1959. They are also partly the result of the author's correspondence with Mr. Jan Maegaard of Copenhagen.

The Libretto

The original text of the libretto of the opera (including the text of Scene 1 of the unfinished third act), and a translation by Mr. Allen Forte, will be found on pp. 112–205. Mr. Hamburger makes free use of Mr. Forte's *singers'* translation in the text of the book, and departs from it only in the interests of literalness.

For me the only exposition deserving the name of analysis is that which brings out the idea of a work and shows how it has been presented and developed.

ARNOLD SCHOENBERG

I

Arnold Schoenberg

Arnold Schoenberg was born in Vienna on September 13, 1874. After teaching himself to start with, he was later encouraged in his musical studies by his future brother-in-law, the conductor and composer Alexander von Zemlinsky, who was two years his senior. In 1891, Schoenberg became a bank clerk; but four years later he freed himself of this tie in order to devote himself entirely to music. In gaining his independence, however, Schoenberg had to face serious difficulties. He directed a workers' choir and orchestrated popular song-hits and operettas. In 1901, he moved to Berlin on his engagement as conductor of Ernst von Wolzogen's *Überbrettl* at the Buntes Theater; and soon after this he obtained a post as teacher of composition at the Sternsche Konservatorium. In mid-1903, Schoenberg returned to Vienna. There now followed the years in which his first pupils gathered round him—among them Alban Berg, Anton von Webern and Erwin Stein—and in which he formulated the ideas in his *Harmonielehre* (published in 1911). It was at this time, too, that Schoenberg first appeared in public as a composer, and that the gulf between his music and that of his contemporaries, and therefore the gulf between himself and the general public, widened increasingly. In 1910, Schoenberg was permitted to hold composition courses at the Vienna Academy of Music. A year later he moved back to Berlin and lectured at the Sternsche Konservatorium. Although Schoenberg the composer was a highly controversial figure, performances of his works became more and more frequent, both at home and abroad. He now began to conduct his own works, and in 1912, the year the symposium *Der blaue Reiter*, to which he had contributed, came out, there appeared the first book about him. In 1908, Schoenberg had begun to paint, and Wassily Kandinsky wrote this of Schoenberg the painter: 'in each of Schoenberg's pictures the inner intention of the artist finds its appropriate form of expression'.

The period before the First World War was one of the most exciting of the century. An epoch of emancipation, these years produced artists who were radical in their rejection of tradition, resolute in desiring the new, perspicacious in formulating their aesthetic theories, and uncompromising in breaking with convention, artists who made no concessions to the public for the sake of success.

During the war, Schoenberg served twice in the army (1915–16 and 1917); he then resumed teaching in Vienna, and his circle of pupils steadily increased. In 1918, the Verein für musikalische Privataufführungen ('Society for the private performance of music') was founded; under Schoenberg's chairmanship, this aimed at producing exemplary performances. For the most part Schoenberg spent the years of crisis after the war in Vienna. In 1925, he was invited to take over the master class for composition at the Prussian Academy of Arts in Berlin as successor to Busoni. Since 1918 Berlin had become the centre of the musical world, a town of intrepid spirits and free discussion. The teaching syllabus of the Academy allowed Schoenberg to arrange his working hours according to his own requirements, and consequently he was able to spend lengthy periods in the south between his periods of teaching.

In May 1933, Schoenberg left Berlin; in September, he was dismissed from his post at the Berlin Academy in violation of his contract. He then left Germany and went briefly to Paris. After having renounced his Jewish faith in 1898, and having been admitted to the Protestant church, Schoenberg now openly recanted and on July 24 he rejoined the Jewish faith and the Jewish community. He proceeded to the United States, living at first in Boston, and then in New York, and dividing his work as a teacher between these two towns. A year later he moved to California on account of his health; he lived at Brentwood, working in Los

Angeles. Once more, teaching provided his means of existence, but he also lectured, directed concerts, and published essays and theoretical writings. In 1935 he began teaching at the University of Southern California, but soon changed this post for a similar one at the University of California in Los Angeles, which he held until his retirement in 1944. After that, private teaching helped to augment his small pension. In 1946, Schoenberg survived a dangerous illness, which, however, left his eyesight considerably impaired. His last years, taken up by further composition and theoretical work, were enriched by growing recognition in the United States—Schoenberg was elected a member of the American National Institute for Arts and Literature in 1947—and by the resumption of old contacts and friendships in a post-war Europe, which, as Schoenberg felt, was now more ready to understand him. Schoenberg died in the night of July 13–14, 1951, at his home in Los Angeles, at the age of seventy-six. A few days before, on July 2, an extract from his opera *Moses and Aaron* had been given its first concert performance at Darmstadt under the direction of Hermann Scherchen.

II

The Religious Element in Schoenberg's Work

Throughout his life Schoenberg was active as composer, musical theorist, writer on music, essayist and painter. Everything served him as a means of communication; indeed, his form of universal productivity reminds us of the type of romantic artist whose ideal was the 'unity of all the arts'. The second edition (1921) of Schoenberg's *Harmonielehre* contains this revealing statement: 'The laws that govern a man of genius are those that will govern future generations of men.' This may be supplemented by similar quotations. Robert Schumann wrote, 'artists are prophets', and Beethoven spoke of 'the heavenly art which alone is the mainspring of that strength that enables me to devote the best part of my life to the Muses' (1824). The 'word of God' is manifest in the 'creations of genius', Liszt wrote to Wagner in 1852; and as early as 1885, Hugo Wolf had had the same thought as Schoenberg: 'The comet course of a genius cannot be deflected into traditional paths. Genius creates order and elevates its will to a law.' In 1896, Gustav Mahler told Anna Mildenburg that he was working on a 'great opus'. 'It claims one's whole personality; often one is so deeply involved that one is quite dead to the world outside oneself. One becomes as it were an instrument played upon by the universe. At such times I no longer belong to myself. . . .' Richard Wagner repeatedly speaks of his isolation. Thus to Friedrich Nietzsche (1872): 'In general, I have the prevailing sensation of knowing less and less of my contemporaries; this may be inevitable for one who creates for posterity. The loneliness of the individual is boundless.' Mahler thought of himself as the instrument of the universe, while Alexander Scriabin thought of himself as 'absolute being' (*Promethean Phantasies*, 1900–1905).

First Beethoven, then Schumann, Wagner and Liszt, and then Scriabin and Schoenberg—all these artists speak of the composer as a being of a special order. He is a genius, he has a mission to fulfil, he is the harbinger of another, supra-mundane world, which is often equated with the concept of divinity; he is a prophet. He is put above ordinary mortals, and elevated to bring them light. He is a Promethean figure. He lives as an example to men, towering above them. He is in advance of his age. His path is lonely but he must pursue it. Only later ages will understand him, honour and emulate him, will perceive his genius, recognize him as a prophet, and make a cult of him; for in his lifetime he is appreciated only by the few, a circle of close friends who are his pupils and disciples, revering him as master.

This cult of the creative artist began in the second half of the eighteenth century. In music it reached its absolute climax with Richard Wagner; but there was a marked return to it in the years before the outbreak of the First World War when on the surface Europe seemed to be a secure world, while beneath could be seen the signs of dissolution, of approaching collapse and a new order of things. The great wave of Expressionism could be interpreted as a new departure, a premonition of things to come. Schoenberg stood at the centre of this age, registering its musical currents with the sensitivity of a seismograph.

Arnold Schoenberg's *oeuvre*, arranged as it is in continuous and nearly correct chronological order by the composer's own opus-numbers, consists of fifty works and groups of works; not included in this list are the unfinished opera *Moses and Aaron*, the unfinished oratorio *Die Jakobsleiter*, the *Gurrelieder*, and his arrangements of works by other composers. The fifty numbered compositions include vocal and instrumental works in about equal proportions.

In a letter of 1922 Schoenberg wrote that at no time in his life had he been 'anti-religious', or even 'un-religious'. A glance at the texts of the vocal works shows us that Schoenberg was always concerned with religious, ethical and philosophical subjects. In the chronological grouping of these works, a rhythm is clearly discernible; a sequence of seven plus seven years, and a culmination at about every fifteenth year. 1907 was the year of the *a cappella* chorus *Friede auf Erden* ('Peace on Earth'), Op. 13 (Conrad Ferdinand Meyer), as well as the second string quartet in F sharp minor which employs a voice for the words of the George poems *Litanei* and *Entrückung*. In the war years 1915–17, Schoenberg wrote the poem for the oratorio *Die Jakobsleiter*; later he began its composition, having already sketched at the end of 1914 or the beginning of 1915 an orchestral scherzo which was subsequently to find a place in the oratorio. This work is the first culminating point in Schoenberg's struggle with the religious world.

The poetic conception of the opera *Moses and Aaron* was preceded by the writing of a drama (hitherto unpublished) called *Der biblische Weg* ('The Biblical Way'). This was written in 1926–27. The composition of the opera *Moses and Aaron*, which belongs to the years 1930–32, is the climax of Schoenberg's lifework and, at the same time, its second culminating point. In America in 1938, Schoenberg set to music the traditional *Kol Nidre*, the prayer for the eve of the Jewish Day of Atonement. In 1945 he again turned his attention to the oratorio *Die Jakobsleiter*.

In the last years, after his grave illness, he never ceased to be concerned with religious subjects.

The publication of the correspondence between Schoenberg and the poet Richard Dehmel throws light on Schoenberg's plans, and particularly on those for 1912. On December 13, 1912, Schoenberg wrote to the poet from Berlin-Zehlendorf saying that he had long been thinking about an oratorio on the following lines: 'modern man, who has passed through materialism, socialism, anarchy, who is an atheist yet has held on to a residue of his old faith (in the form of superstition); this modern man strives with God (cf. *The wrestling Jacob* by Strindberg), and eventually finds God and becomes religious. He learns to pray! A change of heart not to be brought about by a dramatic event, or a calamity, or, least of all, a love-story. These, at most, could only be a background, motivating and propelling the plot. Above all, it should be in modern man's idiom of speech, thought, and expression; it should show the problems that oppress us. For those in the Bible who strive with God also express themselves as people of their age; they speak of their affairs and conform to the social and mental standards of their environment. They are therefore good artistic subjects; yet they cannot be characterized by a present-day composer who is committed to his task. At first I intended writing the poem myself. Now I no longer have the confidence to do it. Then I thought of making a libretto out of Strindberg's *The wrestling Jacob*. Finally, I decided to begin with a positive religious attitude, and arrange the final chapter of Balzac's *Seraphita* entitled "The Ascension".'

How strong Schoenberg's affinity with the world of religion must have been in the years before, during, and after the First World War, is proved by a letter written in 1922 to Wassily Kandinsky. Schoenberg starts by writing of the enormous difficulties of day-to-day existence ('starvation!'). He continues: 'But worst, perhaps, is the overthrow of everything one once believed in.' He goes on to speak of 'another, higher faith' upon which he has increasingly learnt to depend. 'My poem *Die Jakobsleiter* would make it clear to you what I mean: it is religion, though without the fetters of organization. In these years religion has been my only support—I confess that here for the first time.'

The third culminating point began in 1945, and it produced *The Prelude to Genesis* (1945), the cantata *A Survivor from Warsaw* (1947), and the triptych contained in Op. 50; the third section of Op. 50, the *Modern Psalms*, occupied Schoenberg in the last days before his death.

These periods in Schoenberg's work tell us, it is true, something about the creative rhythm of his life, but more instructive is the actual transformation of thought and faith. Conrad Ferdinand Meyer's poem *Friede auf Erden* ('Peace on Earth') is wholly conceived in the Christian spirit of 'glad tidings', of the everlasting hope of peace on earth. Stefan George's *Entrückung* ('Transfiguration'), on the other hand, is born of a pantheistic creed; given to a soprano voice, it forms the finale of the second string quartet, Op. 10 ('ich fühle luft von anderem planeten . . . ich bin ein funke nur von heiligen feuer, ich bin ein dröhnen nur der heiligen stimme') ('I sense the air of another planet . . . only a spark am I of the sacred fire, an echo of the eternal voice'). In a pantheistic vein, too, is the poem *Natur* ('Nature') by Heinrich Hart which was used by Schoenberg in the first of his *Six Songs for Voice and Orchestra*, Op. 8.

Very different are the spiritual worlds that had opened up for Schoenberg when he wrote the text of the oratorio *Die Jakobsleiter*. It can be shown that Schoenberg was stimulated by reading Balzac's *Seraphita*, a story into which the French novelist introduces Swedenborg's mystical theology. It is also possible that Schoenberg may have studied theosophical writings. These stimuli were absorbed in the drama *Die glückliche Hand* ('The Hand of Fate') (composed 1910–13), *Die Jakobsleiter*, and the poems *Totentanz der Prinzipien* ('Death-dance of Principles') and *Requiem*. The idea of reincarnation here becomes the centre of religious faith.

The oratorio *Die Jakobsleiter* is a vision of the time-interval in the other world between death and reincarnation, expressed in dialogues between choruses and individual souls, and the arch-angel Gabriel, who here appears as judge and counsellor, until towards the end God himself speaks. Throughout, the individual stands for the whole: 'the called one', 'the rebellious one', 'the wrestler', 'the chosen one', 'the monk', 'the dying man'. After a great symphonic interlude, Gabriel bids them make themselves ready for reincarnation. Now begins the second part of the work, the exchanges between the souls on the one hand, and the demons, genii, stars, gods and angels on the other; this in turn leads into the tripartite final scene, a chorus from the depths, a main chorus, and a chorus from on high forming a vast concerted invocation of the gift of God's grace, 'eternal love and blessedness'.

The text of *Die Jakobsleiter* is intended for repeated reading, perusal, and thought. Its subject-matter is comprehensive enough to fill entire theological volumes. Indeed, the weakness of the text lies in its vacillation between operatic libretto, sermon, contemplation and theological exegesis—an unfortunate misjudgment of Schoenberg's that sheds light on some problematical traits in his character. Yet this negative impression is entirely obliterated by the music. The score had a fate of its own. In the summer of 1917, Schoenberg, under the impulse of inspiration, wrote the first half of the work in short-score. Interrupted by his army service, he never again succeeded in finding a spontaneous continuation that might have led to the completion of the work, despite repeated attempts. The existing sketch has been worked out by Winfried Zillig. It was first performed in Vienna in 1961 at a special concert in connection with the festival of the International Society for Contemporary Music.

A highly significant composition, one of Schoenberg's great works, has thus become known to the world. Written at the peak of Expressionism, this music lays open all the heights and depths of which emotion is capable. But the work's emotional extremes and its vivid orchestral colours are bound together in great formal structures. Powerful choruses, whose dramatic impact anticipates *Moses and Aaron*, are found next to moving solo-scenes. Very much in the style of the period are the melodramatic manner of declamation and the expressionistic feverishness of the work's emotional world. There can be no doubt that *Die Jakobsleiter* is the greatest work of this particular period in Schoenberg's output. In the future, it will take its place by *Moses and Aaron*. There is one passage in the work, however, that is unique in Schoenberg's entire *oeuvre*: the end of the musical torso. It contains a representation of death, dissolution and transfiguration. A woman on her death-bed describes her transition from life to death, she becomes disembodied, she feels that she is floating upwards. The music here reaches the realms of the spirit, the realms of transfiguration. The speaking-voice becomes a singing-voice, winging its way upwards on wordless sounds. Distant orchestras are heard through loudspeakers distributed over the hall. The spheres begin to reverberate.

These theological beliefs were not without influence on the idea of, and the formulation of, the twelve-note principle, the beginnings of which go back to the end of December 1914, or to January 1915. Swedenborg's concept of Heaven—Balzac's description does not allow for time and space in eternity—corresponds to Schoenberg's 'principle of absolute and unified experience of musical space', a concept which is realized through the note-row, the basic set and its modifications. The 'method of composing with twelve notes'—this is how Schoenberg described the twelve-note principle—is not an exclusively musical method, or merely theoretical speculation, or a historical consequence of the situation of 1910. Not just a single idea, it is the sum of all experiences, based on a religious outlook. The *Four Songs for Voice and Orchestra*, Op. 22, composed in 1913–16, was the last work to be completed before a creative pause of several years. The songs are based on texts of supra-denominational religious trends: *Seraphita* by Ernest Dowson (translated into German by Stefan George), and three poems by Rilke: 'Alle welche dich suchen' ('All that seek thee') and 'Mach mich zum Wächter deiner Weiten' ('Let me be the guardian of thy realms') from the *Stundenbuch* ('Book of Hours'); and *Vorgefühl* ('Premonition') ('Ich bin wie eine Fahne von Fernen umgeben': 'Like a flag, I am surrounded by distances') from the *Buch der Bilder* ('Book of Images').

The *Vier Stücke für gemischten Chor* ('Four pieces for mixed chorus'), Op. 27, were written in 1925. The first two of these are settings of original words; they are not poetry, but rhythmical prose; in them we do not find subjectivism, but ethical tenets; we do not find lyricism, but religious imperatives. Op. 27, No. 2, 'Du sollst nicht, du musst' ('Thou shalt not, thou must') is already formulating the basic theological idea of *Moses and Aaron* when it says: 'Thou shalt not make an image. . . . An image asks for names . . . Thou shalt believe in the Spirit, thou must, chosen one. . . .' In this choral work there is as yet no direct reference to the Old Testament. It was a few years later in his drama *Der biblische Weg* ('The Biblical Way'), written in 1926–27, and in *Moses and Aaron*, that Schoenberg discovered the world of the Old Testament. From there it was only a short step to the public avowal of his Judaism in Paris in 1933; a formal declaration of his faith and reunion with the Jewish community.

In this context, a letter which Schoenberg wrote on May 4, 1923, to his old friend Kandinsky, is of importance. This letter is by no means a theological defence of Judaism, but a purely human vindication invoking the dignity of mankind, and of Judaism, against the vague generalized accusations and the various forms of abuse levelled at it. With regard to Schoenberg's return to the Jewish faith, a letter to Alban Berg, his friend and pupil, contains essential information. The letter was written from Paris in October 1933. 'As you must surely have noticed, my return to the Jewish faith occurred long ago, and is discernible even in the published sections of my work ('Thou shalt not, thou must') as well as in *Moses and Aaron*, of which you have known since 1928, but which goes back for at least another five years; it is particularly noticeable in my drama *The Biblical Way*, which was conceived in 1922 or 1923 but not finished until 1926–27.'

According to David Josef Bach, the drama *The Biblical Way* shows 'the right way, that is, the way of the Bible. God has revealed it.' The protagonist Max Arun's plans for founding a new Palestine come to nothing because of his human imperfections, and it is only by a martyr's death that the hero is able eventually to achieve the degree of perfection possible for him. Max Arun represents the Jewish people. In himself he unites the two personalities, Moses and Aaron, that were to be separated in the opera: Moses, the idea; Aaron, the word. In a letter, Schoenberg mentions briefly that the drama deals with the 'emergence of the Jews as a people'.

In his later religious works Schoenberg has moved completely into the world of the Old Testament. However, only one of those works has a direct liturgical basis: the *Kol Nidre* of 1938. In a letter written by Schoenberg in 1941 to Paul Dessau, we are told of the compositional problems that faced him when he set out to use the 'traditional melody' of the *Kol Nidre*; for this is not a 'melody' in our sense of the term, but a number of juxtaposed phrases of a monodic, i.e. a unisonal and linear, character.

De Profundis, a setting in Hebrew of Psalm 130 for six-part *a capella* chorus, completed on July 2, 1950, is based on the actual words of the Bible. The cantata, *A Survivor from Warsaw* (1947), to a text by Schoenberg in which the persecuted Jews intone the *Shema Yisroel*, is an avowal of Judaism and humanity, of the nobility of suffering and of the overcoming of adversity by suffering. The *Prelude*, Op. 44, composed in 1945 for orchestra and mixed choir (the latter singing vowels only), presents a theological view of God and the world, a description of the universe before the act of creation. The last group of compositions contains, as mentioned, the setting of Psalm 130 (Op. 50 B), and a four-part mixed chorus *Dreimal tausend Jahre* ('Three times a thousand years'), Op. 50 A, to words by Dagobert D. Runes. The poet sings of the temple of Jerusalem, while the psalms, sounding softly from the mountains, proclaim the promised advent of God.

Opus 50 C forms an independent poetic musical work, called by Schoenberg *Modern Psalms*. The text consists of two groups. The first ten psalms were written between September 1950 and February 1951; a second group, begun on March 23, 1951, goes up to the sixth psalm which was begun on July 3, ten days before Schoenberg's death, and remained unfinished. Schoenberg's psalms cannot be compared to those of the Bible. They are neither songs of praise nor prayers, but the great confessions of an individual, a testament to posterity, a posthumous torso which Schoenberg was not able to complete or round off. They are predominantly reflective: God's almightiness, prayer, hope, an enquiry into the justice of God, the idea of grace, the self as part of the community of the chosen people—these are the themes commented upon by Schoenberg from the viewpoint of the Old Testament. He then extends his viewpoint and meditates on belief in mysteries, miracles, and the ten commandments which 'today have already become the foundation of morality, ethics and jurisdiction in almost all nations of a higher civilization, and which, one day, will enlighten all the peoples of the world'. Schoenberg then turns his thoughts to Jesus, charity, the faith of children, love, and the procreative instinct, and, finally, to prayer again, and the duties of the Jews in their role as the chosen people. His last recorded thoughts seem to be intended as a further enquiry into the question of the religious determination of moral values.

The manuscript of the first psalm bears the date of its inception, October 2, 1950. Of this 86 bars are extant: they are the dialogue of a human being with God. 'Who am I?' is the outcry of a creature seized by mystical awe at the vision of the 'only one, eternal one, all-powerful one, all-knowing one, inconceivable one'. The last words set to music by Schoenberg are 'And yet I pray as all that lives prays'. The composition remained unfinished.

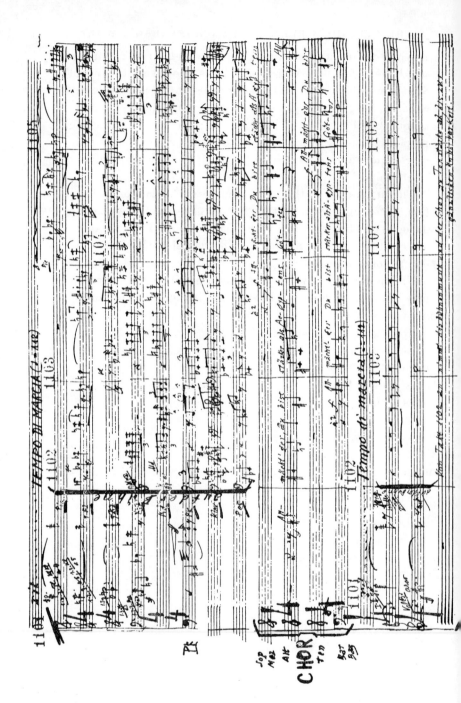

III

'Moses and Aaron',
the Spiritual World

Act I, Scene I: 'The Calling of Moses'

The opera begins with the entry of six solo voices behind closed curtains. When the scene is revealed, we see Moses (a speaking role) before the Burning Bush in the desert, and hear him addressing God thus: 'Only one, infinite, Thou omnipotent one, unperceived and inconceivable God'.

Then God, the Voice from the Burning Bush, speaks to Moses: 'Here lay your shoes aside. You stand on ground that is holy. Be God's prophet!' Moses pleads with God to spare him this task; he points to the burden of his years and the feebleness of his tongue; at last, however, he silently accepts his mission, which is to free his people from the abominations of Egypt; for that is God's will. He shall convince his people by miracles, and Aaron shall be his mouthpiece. For this is what God promises him: 'Your people were the chosen ones before all others, they are the folk of the one God alone. . . . I shall conduct you forward to where with the infinite oneness you shall be a model to every nation'. He shall meet his brother Aaron in the desert. 'Go forth now!' is the final, just as it is the first, exhortation of the Voice from the Burning Bush.

Moses calls upon the God of his fathers: 'God of Abraham, Isaac and Jacob who has once more awakened their great thoughts in my own mind'. Moses has been chosen by God to proclaim His name to His people and to liberate His people, in the name of God, from their Egyptian bondage. His mandate is divine, and at the same time national, and with it there descends on him the blessing and the curse of a prophet's fate. Moses knows himself to be of a strong faith. But can he re-awaken, in a people that has lost the knowledge of its paternal god, the idea of a divinity of which it must not make any image? 'Aaron shall be your mouth,' says God.

In the first scene Moses is alone with his God, in the second he is alone with his brother.

Act I, Scene II:
'Moses meets Aaron in the Wasteland'

Aaron (tenor) has followed God's bidding and is coming to meet his brother in the desert. He is filled with gratitude towards God and love for his people, and—in contrast to the serious, ponderous Moses—is eager to undertake the task ordained by God. But he draws back and asks the timid question: 'People, chosen by the only one, can you worship what you dare not even conceive?' 'How can fantasy thus picture the unimaginable?' retorts Moses, when Aaron speaks of God in the following words: 'O vision of highest fantasy, how glad it is that you've enticed it to form you!' Moses gravely admonishes his brother: 'Purify your thinking, free it from worthless things, let it be righteous. No other reward is given your offerings.' The scene closes with the brothers' voices heard once more together; Aaron's in prayer, 'Almighty one, be the god of this people, release them from Pharaoh's bondage!' and Moses' saying the words, 'Law of thought irresistibly forces fulfilment.'

Aaron's buoyant enthusiasm ends with this softly uttered prayer; Moses' faith is immutable: for him the knowledge of God is a law that has to be lived. It is the inexorability of this law that he has to proclaim to his people.

The brothers had been alone with their thoughts; now, to carry out their mission, they have to meet the people. And so the third character in the opera enters, the people who are forever torn from one extreme to the other, unbelieving and pious, inert and inflammable, spiteful and devout, phlegmatic and fanatical. Some individuals stand out from the mass: a priest (bass), faithful to the old gods, conservative and sober-minded, and, on the other side, three fanatics of the new faith: a young girl (soprano), a young man (tenor), and another man (baritone).

Act I, Scenes III and IV: 'Moses and Aaron bring God's Message to the People'

The girl and the two men report that they saw Aaron 'just as a fiery flame sprang forth' bidding him go to Moses in the desert. To Moses, who has slain Pharaoh's taskmaster and fled, while vengeance overtook the people? What can come from Moses but renewed unrest? 'A new god: new sacrifices!'

Now the people are divided into two groups. One is hostile: 'Who is this who would mightier be than Pharaoh's gods?' The other, led by three adherents of the newly announced god, is enthusiastic: 'We want to make offerings! We want to give worship! He shall make us free!' In dull resignation to its fate, the first group is about to return to work when Moses and Aaron are seen approaching in the distance. The people now describe the brothers' appearance: Moses, his rod in his hand, his white head mighty, and his arm powerful, is advancing slowly; Aaron's step is light and winged.

Act I, Scene IV

Moses and Aaron are assailed by all the people with questions about the new god. The mob is excited and ready to sacrifice everything to him: 'Self-love compels us to make offerings; giving oneself is pleasure, the highest favour!'

But the crowd becomes serious and is roused to opposition as the brothers lift up their voices. Moses speaks of God: He is 'the only one, infinite, inconceivable'; He 'demands no offering from you; He wants not a part, but the whole'. Aaron proclaims the promise of God: 'On your knees, then, to worship Him!'

But where is this god? Worship him? Whom? 'Show him to us.' Aaron explains to the people that God is invisible. 'He, your most mighty of gods, cannot show Himself before us?' And when Aaron retorts that only the righteous shall see Him, he is answered with ironical laughter.

Then Moses tonelessly utters these words: 'Almighty one, now my strength is exhausted, and my thoughts become powerless in Aaron's word!'

For during this tumultuous crowd-scene, the first act of the spiritual drama between Moses and Aaron has already silently taken place—a drama of which the seed had been sown in the colloquy of the brothers in the desert.

Moses has been unable to make himself understood, Aaron's words have found no response, their mission has apparently failed. But suddenly Aaron, wrenching the rod from Moses, demands: 'Silence! The word is mine and the deed!' He is still acting in the name of God, for the six solo voices from the first scene call to him in command, 'Aaron!' He transforms the rod into a snake, demagogically making the most of the terror that grips the people: 'In Moses' hand a rigid rod: this, the law; in my own hand the most supple of serpents: discretion. Now stand so, as it commands!' The people, convinced by the miracle-working power of his God, now recognize Aaron as their master. There follows a hymn of rejoicing.

For a second time we hear the six solo voices; softly they sing the consonant 'm'. Aaron is now intent on restoring to the people belief in their own power. 'Moses' heart is now like your own, because he knows you lack spirit. Placing his hand on the heart that is sick just as yours is, see!' The second miracle occurs. Moses' hand becomes leprous. 'Therein see yourselves: for your spirit shall defeat the hosts of Pharaoh!' Once more, the hymn resounds; it culminates in the exultant cry 'Almighty God!' and leads on to the angry shouts of 'Everything for freedom! Kill the taskmasters! Destroy their idols! Off to the wasteland!'

But the priest bars their way: 'Madmen! How can the waste-land nurture you?' Moses replies: 'In the wasteland, pureness of thought will provide you nurture, sustain you and advance you . . .', and Aaron develops this thought by deflecting it into an enticing promise: '. . . and the eternal one lets you see an image of your earthly good fortune in every spiritual marvel'. His words become more and more seductive: 'The almighty one can change mere sand to fruit, fruit to gold, gold to rapture, rapture to spirit'. In the name of this godhead, Aaron works a third miracle; he changes Nile-water into blood, and with an ardent persuasiveness he incites the people against the Egyptians. In solemn, rapt tones he proclaims God's promise to the people (the six solo voices confirm this: 'Chosen people!'), and predicts the downfall of Pharaoh.

The second promise of God ('I shall conduct you forward to where with the infinite oneness you shall be a model for every nation') is wilfully changed by Aaron into a promise of mere creature comfort: 'He will then lead you to a land where milk and honey flow.'

Enraptured, the people respect Aaron's words, and in a magnificent climax the hymn is resumed; and the first act closes in a mood of religious ecstasy, national fanaticism and deceptive hopes for the future.

Moses, to whom the word is not given, has failed. The drama between the two brothers ends here with Aaron's victory.

Between the first and second act there lies the exodus of the people from Egypt, the destruction of the Egyptian host in the Red Sea, and the journey through the desert.

Moses has retreated to the wilderness of Mount Sinai and has given strict orders that nobody should approach the mountain. The people are full of uncertainty. This situation is reflected in the

Interlude

A small choir, placed before the curtain, in darkness, expresses doubt and hopelessness in its questions: 'Where is Moses? Abandoned are we! Where is his god?'

Act II, Scenes I and II:
'Aaron and the Seventy Elders before the Mountain of Revelation'

The seventy elders, spokesmen of the people, press Aaron with questions. Forty days have passed since Moses has left them. Violence is rife among the tribes, the people are desperate. Trying to avoid an answer, Aaron puts the elders off. At the beginning of Scene Two, 'the roaring crowd, in furious agitation, rushes upon the stage from all directions', calling on Aaron for a reckoning. In face of this onslaught Aaron becomes unsure of himself. 'My brother Moses dwells upon that summit, close to his god . . . maybe his god has now left him . . . it may be that he has killed him.' But the people demand the death of the 'priesthood serving this false god'. In despair, the seventy elders call upon Aaron to give in. Yet it is not only the hopelessness of the situation, but Aaron's character itself that leads him to this fatal change of mood. With an impressive gesture, he turns to the people: 'I return your gods to you . . . to you, the gods have ever-present and always common substance. . . . Bring out your gold! Yield it!' The mood of the roaring crowd is quickly transformed into one of jubilation.

Act II, Scene III: 'The Golden Calf and the Altar'

The stage is revealed, and the image of the Golden Calf comes into view. Aaron gives a theological explanation. According to him, the image attests 'that in all things that are, a god lives'; gold, the image's substance, is the principle of immutability; the figure itself, on the other hand, is the image, is perceptible and changeable. 'Revere yourselves in this symbol!' So he inveigles his people to self-deification, to glorification of the temporal, and to adoration of perpetual transience.

The people, led by Aaron, have deserted God. The following scenes represent idolatry, and the hours of estrangement from God. Yet even these do not lack a certain greatness, since they are informed with a feeling of tribal solidarity. A heathen celebration that ends with an orgy, unfolds before our eyes.

Preparations are made for the sacrifice: cattle are led on, and burnt offerings are made; the slaughterers close their ranks for the dance. A sick woman is carried in and placed in front of the Golden Calf. There are miraculous cures. Beggars put their rags on the altar, old men commit suicide before the Golden Calf.

A fanfare heralds the arrival of the tribal leaders and the Ephraimite. They come galloping in, dismount in front of the Golden Calf and pay homage to it. At this moment a youth appears who is known to us from the first act as a follower of the new faith. In vain he tries to restrain the assembled people from their idolatry. The tribal leaders slay him.

Wine is flowing in torrents. Drunkenness infects the crowd, and they begin to dance. The seventy elders comment on the scene in agitated voices. Four virgins—one of them possibly the young girl of the first act—are ready to sacrifice themselves. The priests kill them, after a long embrace, by plunging their knives into their hearts; the blood is gathered and poured on the altar.

The last scene, an orgy of destruction, immolation and sexual frenzy, begins with wild dances, and continues until the sacrificial fires have died down.

Act II, Scene IV

A voice is heard from afar: 'Moses is descending from the mountain!' Moses appears, holding the Tables of the Law, and in extreme wrath he hurls these words at the Calf: 'Begone, you symbol of powerlessness to enclose the boundless in a finite image!'

Act II, Scene V: 'Moses and Aaron'

There begins now the great dispute between the brothers which is to end with the triumph of Aaron and the collapse of Moses. Aaron tries, at first timidly, to justify himself. He had only carried out his task of working miracles before the people; he had heard the inner voice, and, in Moses' absence, had given the people an image. In towering rage, Moses counters: 'God's eternity destroys the idol's presence! No image this, no miracle! This is the law. The immutable is proclaimed, though it be as temporal as these tables in your mouth.' Aaron, gaining in confidence, retorts that the endurance of Israel testifies to the idea of a timeless God, and that he, Aaron, loves his people: 'I live for them and want to sustain them.' 'For the sake of the spirit!' Moses interrupts. 'No people is faithful unless it feels,' Aaron replies. But while Moses remains inflexible—'They must grasp the idea! They live for that end!'—Aaron confirms his conviction that the idea must be presented to the people in a manner suitable for its comprehension. For Moses this is a falsification, and when Aaron refers to the Tables of the Law as 'images also, only parts of the whole idea', Moses, in sudden despair, smashes the Tables and asks God to withdraw the task given to him. His brother's weakness now gives Aaron the upper hand. A pillar of fire appears in the sky, changing at daybreak into a pillar of cloud. The people, newly aroused by this wonder, pass by in the background; they know themselves to be the chosen people once again, and raise up their voices in a hymn of freedom. Aaron experiences the triumph of his power: 'Thus through me has God given a signal to the people, . . . a god-sent sign like the Burning Bush. The infinite thus shows not Himself, but shows the way to Him and the way to the promised land!' Slowly, Aaron walks to the back of the stage.

Moses stays alone as the chorus disappears behind the scene. How is it possible for God to allow this interpretation? 'Shall Aaron, my mouth, fashion this image?' Where does the word of

God end and magic begin? He is unable to recognize the dividing line, and is forced to conclude: 'Then I have fashioned an image, too, false as an image must be! Thus am I defeated! Thus, all was but madness that I believed before, and can and must not be given voice. O word, thou word that I lack!' In despair he sinks to the ground.

Although Moses has lost faith in his own strength, he has retained his belief in God, whom he acknowledges as the only one, eternal, omnipresent, invisible and inconceivable. And so he regains his strength and is soon able to follow his call once more.

Act III: 'Aaron's Death'

Moses, having ordered Aaron to be put in fetters, again calls him to account, this time in the presence of witnesses, the seventy elders. He accuses him of being bound by the world of images, and of failing to understand the spiritual power of miracles: 'You speak more simply than you understand, for you know that the rock is, like the wasteland and the Burning Bush, an image . . . thus you won the people not for the eternal one, but for yourself.' Aaron again defends himself by saying that he wanted to win the trust of the people 'for their freedom so that they would become a nation'. Moses replies: 'To serve the divine idea is the freedom for which this people has been chosen. . . . The god that you showed to them is an image of powerlessness, is dependent upon a power beyond himself, must fulfil what he has promised; must do what he is asked. . . . The almighty one is not committed to anything, is bound by nothing.' And now Moses accuses his brother of betrayal, betrayal to the gods, the betrayal of the idea to images, of the chosen people to other people, of the extraordinary to the commonplace.

'Shall we kill Aaron?' the guards ask Moses.

Moses, however, does not reply, and continues his accusation, now directing it at the seventy elders, and through them at the people of Israel: You are chosen to possess those gifts, to fight for the divine idea. But when you 'go forth among the people' and 'employ those gifts for false and base ends . . . whensoever you had abandoned the wasteland's renunciation and your gifts had led you to the highest summit, then from the splendour of such misuse you were ever hurled back into the wasteland'.

After these prophetic words, Moses bids the warriors untie Aaron's bonds: 'Set him free, and may he live if he can'. Aaron is freed, he stands up, and then falls down dead.

And Moses turns back to the elders: 'But in the wasteland you are invincible and you shall achieve the goal: unity with God'.

IV

The Dialectics of the Idea

Schoenberg took the subject of his opera from the Old Testament. There he found the action: the calling of Moses (*Exodus* 3–4), and the exodus from Egypt and the falling away from God (*Exodus* 32); there he found the religious revelation: God's promise (*Exodus* 3–4), and the laws which God gave to the people through Moses (*Exodus* 20–31); there also he found the spiritual tensions, such as the ambiguousness of Aaron, who is responsible for the worship of the Golden Calf (*Exodus* 32). Occasionally Schoenberg takes over certain phraseology from Luther's translation. The course of the action is made different from that of the Bible solely in order to establish the biblical thought more clearly. Schoenberg's claims for authorship rest above all on the logic and consequentiality with which he has worked out the dialectic between Moses and Aaron. In the Bible the contrast between them is already manifest—because of his disobedience Aaron is punished by God and barred from entering the promised land (*Numbers* 20 and 24). With Schoenberg, on the other hand, both the brothers are protagonists; the spiritual problems are reduced to their basic form, call it what you will: one may describe it as the struggle between spirit and non-spirit, the power of God and magic, law and image, the inconceivable and the visible, worship of God and self-glorification, saintliness and sin, spirit and flesh, and logos and instinct. Schoenberg draws the conclusion that only in the spirit is there life. Human freedom means a life of the spirit. Aaron freed by Moses stands up and then falls dead. He has sinned against God and has himself forfeited his life.

Schoenberg's text should not be judged by literary standards

39

alone. The action and the words are intended as a basis for music, and it is only the unity of the whole, the interplay of action, words and music, that can give one a yardstick by which to judge the work. Equally meaningless is the question whether *Moses and Aaron*, considered as a representative of an artistic *genre*, is an opera or an oratorio. Performances have shown that the work produces the same overpowering impression on the stage as in a concert-performance. It is the ultimate *credo* of a man whose creativity was placed more and more at the service of religion, and who, towards the end of his life, was exclusively occupied with religious thoughts that could only partially be expressed in music. The critical-literary approach to Schoenberg's poem misses its point, as does any attempt to evaluate Schoenberg's other texts in terms of literature. These are not conceived as examples of the art of letters, any more than Richard Wagner's literary productions are meant to stand up to literary scrutiny. Schoenberg was no poet in the usual sense of the word, or when measured by the standards that had been established in German literature. Like Richard Wagner, he wrote poetry for music. Music and words have the same relationship for Schoenberg as Wagner. The musical conception follows the words, shaping them into musical structures. The spiritual idea and its verbal, dramatic expression are primary factors. They inspire the music by suggesting new contexts and novel combinations of the two media, the structure of which is purely musical. Thus, while retaining their spiritual significance, the words are dissolved in the higher amalgam of musical form. This higher unity permits of no separation or isolation of single elements. Here words and music must always be appreciated as a synthesis.

Never before has anything comparable to that of *Moses and Aaron* been seen on the operatic stage. It is a ritual act, and again it is not. The ritual elements are restricted to the first two scenes—the calling of Moses and his meeting with Aaron in the desert. Ritual commitments are almost entirely avoided by Schoenberg, nor does he concern himself with the law-giving of Moses; everything is reduced to the spiritual conception of God which unconditionally informs Moses' life, and which he imposed without compromise on his co-religionists. In this work there are no realms of privacy, no secondary plots. All is dominated by the idea of God, the almighty, eternal and inconceivable one. The action lies in the struggle for this idea, in the deviation from the purity of the notion to the point of aberration, idolatry, and betrayal.

The plot of the opera is of the utmost simplicity. God and Moses on the one hand, and Aaron and the people on the other, are antagonists. The tragic conflict at the end of the second act is brought about by the doubts that assail Moses; not indeed doubts about God, but doubts relating to the contradiction be-tween *his* conception of God, and the things that are done by Aaron in the name of God. All the others are marginal figures, types, characteristic representatives of the stages between belief and unbelief. The people are the ever-vacillating mass. The chorus is never used for reflection, as in oratorio, but always dramatically, as a crowd in action. No single individuals come to the fore; at the most there are groups, but they too are uniform in their attitude.

God's command to Moses reaches the people through Aaron. *Moses and Aaron* is a drama of ideas distilled from the history of religion. It represents the greatest and highest, and at the same time the most difficult, theological task that at any time confronts mankind: the perception of God and, consequent on this, the quest for man's estate in and under eternity. It is only symbolic that at the close Moses addresses his prophetic message to the seventy elders. In reality he is speaking to his people. Moses was alone with his God when he accepted God's mission in the desert. Now, at the end of the opera and alone once more, he confers his mandate on the people.

'Everything I have written', Schoenberg told his friend Alban Berg, 'has a certain inner likeness to myself.' With this remark, Schoenberg defends his conception of the opera *Moses and Aaron* against the imputation of a 'certain similarity' to Strindberg's *Moses*, and he continues: 'My main idea, as well as the many,

many concomitant thoughts that are put forward actually and allegorically—they are all bound up so closely with my person that the possibility of Strindberg having propounded something of even extrinsic similarity does not arise.' A perusal of Strindberg's drama (it was written in 1905 and printed in 1918) proves that there are not even any extrinsic similarities, save certain parallel lines of action which are determined by their biblical source. What is scarcely hinted at by Strindberg, is placed in the centre by Schoenberg: the great antinomy.

'A certain inner likeness to myself': all the same, there is no autobiographical or self-analytical bridge between the work and Schoenberg's own person. 'The subject and its treatment belong entirely to the realm of the philosophy of religion', Schoenberg wrote to Josef Rufer, a few months before his death; and he took strong exception to an article in *Grove's Dictionary of Music and Musicians* in which the antithesis between Moses, embodying the spiritual principle, and Aaron, standing for matter and its restrictions, is compared with that between the artistic conception of Schoenberg's work and its realization in the medium of sound.

About his struggle with the material, i.e. with the contradictions in the Bible, Schoenberg writes thus in a letter of 1933: 'Out of this mighty theme I myself have extracted and put forward the following principal elements: the idea of God the inconceivable, that of the chosen people, and that of the people's leader. My Moses is like Michelangelo's, if only in appearance. He is not at all human. The scene of the Golden Calf signifies a sacrifice of the crowd that wants to abandon the "soulless" faith. As this scene embodies my central idea, I am well on the way to completing it, and it is here that my piece comes closest to being an opera; this is as it should be. My third act, which I am re-modelling, or re-writing, for at least the fourth time, is at the moment still called "The Death of Aaron". Here I have so far been greatly impeded by some contradictions in the Bible that seem almost incomprehensible to me. For although it is only in a few passages that I am keeping strictly to the Bible, it is in just this context that it is rather difficult to overcome such divergencies as "Strike the rock" at one place, and "Speak! . . ." at another. Could you perhaps tell me of some literature that deals with these problems? Up till now, I have tried to find a solution on my own. But these things go on bothering me!'

But let us return to Schoenberg's remark, '. . . it is here that my piece comes closest to being an opera; this is as it should be'. He was certainly thinking of the operatic stage, and of his work's realization on, and by means of, the stage at the time; the effectiveness of this medium must have attracted him. The insight of advancing age may have changed this a little. The 'old Schoenberg's' avowal of Judaism, and its artistic expression and condensation in *Moses and Aaron*, has now taken the form of a *credo*, or 'last will and testament', of prophetic significance. The work's 'stage-effect' is no longer of first importance; but then, even at the time when the opera was first planned, Schoenberg had never thought of the theatre as an end in itself.

V
The Large-scale Musical Structures

The preceding reflections have tried to define the content of the opera, its spiritual tendencies and their realization. Our deliberations were aimed at interpreting the work, not at providing an aesthetic and philosophical rationale. Similarly, the following remarks will be in the character of an exegesis, thus combining analysis and interpretation. Analysis, left to its own devices, merely dissects the music into motives, and in the case of a twelve-note composition, reveals the employment of the series—it is an investigation which fails to enquire into the work's spiritual stature; that is not its concern. Interpretation, on the other hand, tries to perceive the synthesis of details, elevating them to a higher order, and centralizing their spiritual aspects.

Words, action and music form an indivisible whole, and this, in its turn, is subject to the idea of the entire work: the idea of Moses' conception of God and its realization, the discrepancy between idea (law) and image, and the betrayal of the idea and eventual return to idolatry. It is not possible in any single context to separate idea, action, words and music from one another. The attempt, even, would be irresponsible, denying the close unity of the whole. More than that, it would oppose the wish of its creator.

This exposition is intended as an introduction to the work. Its central issues will be dealt with, but not exhaustively. The methods to be employed are indicated by both the work itself and its creator. The reader is recommended to consult the vocal

44

score or the pocket score, and, by his own efforts, to intensify and complement this exposition.

An introduction should be didactic. Let us begin with the observation that the work contains a number of parallel passages, deriving from text and action.

The first words spoken by Moses in the sight of the Burning Bush are the devout description: 'Only one, infinite, thou omnipresent one, unperceived and inconceivable God'. Soft, solemn four-part chords appear in the orchestra (I, bars 8–11).

(The work was provided with bar-numbers by Schoenberg himself. The first act has 970 bars. A new count begins with the Interlude, and runs through to the end of the second act.)

In the second scene, Moses speaks of his God to Aaron in the same words, and Aaron, overawed by the mystery, joins in softly with the words 'Inconceivable God'. The same musical diction recurs here, but the chords are expanded to nine parts (I, bars 183–186). When the brothers meet the people (I, bars 481–483) —Moses proclaiming his idea of God, Aaron, God's promise—the preceding passage from Scene 2 is restated. It returns a fourth time, now reduced to four-part chords (I, bars 833–837) when Moses assures the people: 'In the wasteland, pureness of thought will provide you nurture'. Its last recurrence accompanies the words of the Priest who considers the enigmatic nature of God: 'Unperceivable command from the inconceivable God!'—in nine-part writing, the chords dovetailed, rhythmically and tonally, in the manner of a conundrum (II, bars 60–61, Ex. 13).

Moses, filled with awe before the task that God has imposed on him, stammers out 'My tongue is not flexible. I can think, but not speak' (I, bars 48–53). These bars return, in the same form, when Moses has to admit his weakness in front of the people ('Almighty one, now my strength is exhausted'—I, bars 623–628).

The voice from the Burning Bush promises, 'Aaron shall be your mouth' (I, bars 59–61, Ex. 28). 'Aaron' is the call of the six solo voices when Moses has come to the end of his strength and Aaron begins to play an active role. The chords are repeated here in the same position (I, bars 630–631).

Among the most significant meaningful allusions of this kind is one of the work's leading ideas: the promise of God to the people of Israel 'to be chosen people of the only God' and 'I shall conduct you forward . . .' (I, bars 71–74, and 80–85, Exs. 29 and 30). Aaron transmits these words to the people (I, bars 898–901 and 908–909), who take them up (I, bars 918–922 and 929–930). The parallel passages are note-by-note repetitions; so, too, is the third quotation, at the end of the second act, when the people, seeing the cloudy and fiery pillars, believe in God's forgiveness and know themselves to be the chosen people once more (II, bars 1083–1087 and 1094–1098).

The hymn (Ex. 36) that the people intone three times during the fourth scene of the first act, receives fundamentally the same musical treatment: the main theme, forming a *cantus firmus*, remains the same, as it does also at the hymn's repetition at the end of the second act (I, bars 688–704, 798–813, 936–955, particularly the first three bars; II, bars 1101–1111).

Symbolic ambivalence provides a further parallel: of the first three adherents to the new faith, the youth becomes a martyr, the girl a fanatical worshipper of the Golden Calf, for which she sacrifices herself. It is not without irony that her songs are parallel musical passages, note and pitch being identical: 'I saw him afar' (I, bars 255–264) and 'O golden god' (II, bars 759–768).

The threefold occurrence of the hymn in the first act serves the composer as a means for building a large-scale structure. The hymn is the central section—the refrain—of a musical rondo form.

First miracle (I, bars 630–683)—refrain (*Tempo di marcia*, bars 684–707). The whole structural group is enclosed by the entries of the six solo voices.

Second miracle (bars 716–794)—refrain (bars 794–816); and, subsequently, the dramatic outburst of the chorus 'Everything for freedom' (bars 817–852).

Third miracle (bars 853–917, appended to which is Aaron's pronouncement of God's promise to the people)—repeat of the promise by the people (bars 918–936) and third refrain (bars 936–970; end of the act).

The people, as a protagonist—comparable to the crowd of the Passion—are introduced in the great tableau before Moses and Aaron come on to the stage. The tableau comprises the entire third scene (bars 244–442), and the beginning of the fourth (bars 443–473). In this crowd scene, four solo voices (the girl, the two men, the priest) alternate with a chorus that is, at times, divided into twelve singing or speaking parts. Verbally, and therefore musically, there are two large sections. Their division follows logically from the action: the people are ready to return to their work, when the sight of Moses and Aaron gives a new impetus to their dreams and hopes (first part, bars 244–398, second part, bars 399–473). The first part is a rondo. The refrain is formed by the rapturous utterances of the three soloists, which are contrasted with the cautious, conservative attitude of the Priest. As the three adherents of the new faith gradually succeed in winning over a considerable part of the people until it is split into two opposing factions, the musical texture gradually becomes richer and the contrapuntal treatment—symbolic of the antagonism—is of increasing complexity, while the voice of the priest always remains calm and detached; thus contrast is created between the sections of the rondo form. With the second part, there begins a new polyphonic structure, with new themes, and at bar 443 the exposition of a double fugue.

In a work uncommonly rich in contrapuntal writing, polyphony is never introduced for its own sake, but always serves the dramatic context. Thus the composer is able to maintain the dramatic tension and, at the same time, create large musical structures. The Interlude makes a particularly powerful impact (Ex. 42). Dramatically, it expresses one idea alone: doubt. The various questions that confront the people, as a result of their predicament, are all prompted by doubt but; as themes, they are treated individually. Unity is again ensured by a contrapuntal form: the double fugue. The whole scene is 42 bars long. The listener will scarcely realize that he is experiencing a complex polyphonal masterpiece, so awesome and convincing is the effect of the many interweaving sung and whispered voices; moreover, the rhythmically spoken words are part of the polyphonic web. The movement is *pianissimo* throughout. The orchestra's contribution consists of an agitated rhythmic texture, but so arranged that the incessant unrest has a congealing effect; a symbol of immobility induced by fear and horror.

It would go far beyond the aims of this exposition to examine the canonic writing, the *stretti*, imitations, and all the highly ingenious contrapuntal devices, forms and structures in which the work abounds. Among the large-scale contrapuntal forms is the people's hymn, which is constructed on a *cantus firmus*. This *cantus firmus* (Ex. 36)—so designated by Schoenberg himself—is placed, at its first occurrence, in the baritone voice (I, bars 689–704), at its second (I, bars 798–813) in the mezzo-soprano. A further climax—at the third occurrence (bars 936–955)—is achieved by a strict two-part canon.

These devices, however, are not used in order to divide the music of the opera into distinct musical forms, as is the case in Berg's *Wozzeck*. Schoenberg alternates freely between strict and free forms, according to the demands of the text, and the idea of the work. In free form are the sections of pronounced *arioso* writing that distinguish the part of Aaron, as well as the many bars marked by Schoenberg as 'recitative'. These are 'composed prose', exactly determined as to rhythm and pitch, and yet admitting a certain subjective freedom in execution. The secret of dramatic tension lies, to no small extent, in the significant co-ordination of the work's manifold musical structures.

The scene of 'The Golden Calf and the Altar' is a symphony with solo voices and choruses in five movements. After the short recitative of Aaron (II, bars 308–319), there begins the first, purely orchestral movement (bars 320–454). Its considerable length is supported by a large-scale structure. First, a tremendous upbeat of solemn fanfares (Ex. 1), then another three bars of heavy,

Example 1 (II, bars 320–327)

expansive rhythm. The fanfare at the start of the first and third movements symbolizes the call to the sacrificial feast: 'Tribal leaders, worship with me' in the words of the Ephraimite (II, bars 531–533, Ex. 23). The tempo remains moderate during the first section of the movement (bars 331–370), in which two themes are introduced (Ex. 2 and 3):

Example 2 (II, bars 331–335)

Example 3 (II, bars 335–342)

This music, which accompanies the preparations for the sacrifice, is clearly organized into four sections, *a–b–a–b*. In bars 371 to 396, the tempo increases, and a third theme (Ex. 4) is introduced (on the stage: further preparations, and the first burnt offerings):

Example 4 (II, bars 372–379)

The third section of the movement is formed by 'The Dance of the Slaughterers' (II, bars 397–453), in which themes *a*, *b*, and *c* are developed; its first part shows a decrease, its second an increase of speed.

The second movement of the symphony, the Adagio (II, bars 455–496), accompanies the healing of the sick, the song of the beggars and the suicide of the old men. As a description of pathological behaviour, this music is of a tormented inwardness. Its quality is that of chamber music, the texture being reduced to three or four contrapuntal parts.

The third movement (II, bars 497–597) is again preceded by the fanfare (Ex. 1). Then follows an Allegro in three sections. The entry of the tribal leaders is depicted by impassioned music in march rhythm—at once savage, bold and imposing. Its two themes (Ex. 5 and 6) are:

Example 5 (II, bars 501–503)

Example 6 (II, bars 502–504)

The tempo relaxes for the entry of the voice of the Ephraimite: Schoenberg lends an archaic character to the scene of the twelve tribal leaders. The central part of the movement, the scene of the youth, is treated formally as a contrasting section with different

50

themes (see Ex. 14), and the movement concludes with a brief return of the march.

The fourth movement of the symphony (II, bars 598–823) is a dance movement. It contains the scenes of the sacrificial gifts, the exchange of offerings, and ends with the immolation of the four virgins. After a *grazioso* transition (II, bars 598–605), the basic character of the movement is established by the 'swaying dance tempo'. This 'scherzo' of the symphony is, to bar 758, virtually a single, three-four bar, the thematic roots of which are largely formed by permutations of juxtaposed semi- and whole-tone steps (or vice versa). (See Ex. 22.) At the entry of the virgins, there occurs the already mentioned reminiscence of the first act; with the solo quartet of the virgins, the calm main tempo is resumed. The music accompanying the ritual murder forms the coda of the scene, and as the virgins breathe their last, the main theme (semitone, wholetone, semitone) recurs once more.

Now comes the furious finale, the fifth movement of the symphony (II, bars 824–966). It consists of two parts, the first instrumental, the second with voices—the scenes of excessive idolatry and the people's glorification of their own flesh are succeeded by weariness, by withdrawal, by the coda. The percussion begins, the tempo becomes very taut. No bar is repeated, but here, too, even the smallest detail is structurally determined; thematicism itself is never abandoned. The themes appear as breathless, hectic fragments (Ex. 7).

Example 7 (II, bars 828, 829, 830, 831, 833–835)

It is only in what appears to be a central section (bars 864–880) that intervals larger than an octave are used; from bar 881 on, however, the themes become even more short-winded: savagery is at its peak (Ex. 8).

Example 8 (II, bars 864–868)

When the singing-parts enter (bar 911), the tempo gradually subsides, and now the coda begins. It consists entirely of thematic reminiscences from the whole symphony (bars 914–916=bars 372–374, Ex. 4; bars 929–931=bars 732–734; bars 934–936 quote bars 759–760; bar 951 corresponds to bar 546, etc.). The great arch has been completed.

An impression of particular formal consistency is given by the first two scenes of the opera. 'The Calling of Moses' is a cantata.

The mystical encounter between God and man, the revelation of God, who makes himself known to Moses in the shape of a Burning Bush, who speaks to him from the Bush, takes the form of a dialogue between the voice of God—the six soli and the six-part speaking chorus—and the speaking voice of Moses. There is no action on the stage; music alone holds the field in this movement of 97 bars, and nothing comparable to it exists in the entire literature of music. In its first half, to bar 52, the scene is a dialogue between God and Moses; in the second, God alone speaks, announcing Moses's task and His promise. The whole scene falls into six sections: the infinity of God (bars 1–7); the summoning of Moses (bars 11–15); God's mandate (bars 23–27); the promise to Moses (bars 41–47, 54–70); the promise to the Jewish people (bars 71–85); God's command ('Now be gone hence! Proclaim!' bars 86–97). All this is held together by the musical plan, and by purely musical devices: the first four chords (Ex. 9) which permeate the whole scene, and the two main themes (Ex. 10, 29 and 30) which are closely connected with these same chords.

The second scene, the meeting of the brothers in the waste-land, is quite different. Its integration depends on an alternation of contrasts; these, however, are conceived in purely musical terms and enjoy a high degree of formal unity. There is an introductory orchestral prelude of 25 bars (Ex. 46) which characterizes Aaron, revealing that he is chosen by God; it is a passage of a light, floating character. In bar 124, the dialogue of the brothers begins. In this first section (up to bar 147) their voices are heard simultaneously—Aaron singing, Moses speaking; the orchestra continues with the theme of the introduction. As new themes appear, the dialogue gradually turns into an *arioso* for Aaron; his emphatic manner is expressed by great, soaring *cantilena* passages. And now, the first great rift occurs (bars 178–186, Ex. 26); the contrast between the brothers becomes manifest. The emphatic strain is restated (bars 187–217); but then, to the earnest words of Moses 'Purify your thinking', the second contrasting section emerges (bars 208–217). There follows a third *arioso* for Aaron, in which the main theme of the second *arioso* (Ex. 47) becomes a subsidiary part in the orchestra. The final section of the scene is built on the theme 'Purify your thinking' which now appears in the orchestra. This conclusion alludes significantly to the sequel of the action with its dramatic contrasts.

Just how individual is the reaction of Schoenberg's formal sense to the prevailing mood of the dramatic situation, can also be shown by the great chorus of jubilation which immediately precedes the third scene of the second act, the dance round the Golden Calf. This important turning-point of the dramatic action begins with the cry of the seventy elders, 'Aaron help us! Relent!', followed by Aaron's address. With his last thoughts are mingled the first subdued shouts of joy from the people (II, bars 191–199); these are an introduction to the subsequent choral song in three parts; at the same time, they provide the refrain of the great rondo structure. The first choral song, in three-four time (bars 200–239), has verses that belong to the choral refrain, and song-lines; this gives the following sequence: refrain (bars 200–206); first and second song-line in soprano and bass (bars 207–218); refrain (bars 219–225); third and fourth song-line in alto and tenor (bars 226–232); refrain (bars 233–239). Soon, the shouts shouts of joy are resumed (bars 241–245), now *forte*; then follows the second choral song, in alternating three-four and two-four bars (bars 246–288). In bars 270–273, a rudimentary form of the refrain can be recognized in the orchestra. The third choral song brings the final climax (bars 274–288), the orchestra playing the choral refrain of the first choral song. As an epilogue, the shouts of joy are heard for a third time, now extremely loud (bars 289–307).

Seen as a whole, this scene is a rondo, the first part of which is itself in a rondo-like form.

VI

God as an Idea

$\quad$od as an idea—this concept was taken over by Moses from
his ancestors, to whom God had revealed himself. Infinite
God speaks at the beginning of the opera, while the curtain
is still closed; not in words, but in sound, entrusted to the six
solo voices (Ex. 9):

Example 9 (*I, bars* 1–3)

The chords each have three voices and each is held for three
crotchets. The first and last chord, consisting of an augmented
and a perfect fourth, are the same, allowing for the transposition
of the intervals. The intervallic progression from one chord to
the next is in both cases the same, A to B, the major second.
Rhythmically and dynamically, too, the progressions are
identical.

$\quad$What happens in these first three bars of the opera, before the
entry of the orchestra, never returns in this pure form. It is a
movement of perfect symmetry, a symbol of Him who says of
Himself 'I am the first and I am the last' (*Isaiah* 44, 6).

$\quad$In disclosing Himself to Moses, God emerges from His infinity,
becoming will and thought. At this point a theme arises (Ex. 10),

Example 10 (*I, bars* 11–12)

a self-contained melodic invention of six notes, cast in mirror-form, the fourth, fifth and sixth notes of which (b) are the retrograde of the first three notes (a). Thus the theme becomes a symbol of order and divine will; its significance is enhanced by the step of an augmented fourth between its third and fourth notes. The tritone and its inversion divide the octave into equal parts; no other symmetrical division is possible. In all its imaginable transformations (inversion, retrograde, and retrograde inversion), the theme always retains its individual character as a symbol of eternal, immutable volition. The theme rests in itself. It is entirely linear in conception, free of any harmonic obligation, and invented wholly in the spirit of twelve-note music. Notes 4 to 9 of the twelve-note series are derived from this theme.

The four chords and the six-note theme, as conceived by Schoenberg's artistic imagination, are also a perfect demonstration of what he calls 'the unity of musical space, in which there exists 'no absolute down, no right or left, forward or backward'. In the succession of chords, and in the theme, there is no longer any state of tension, only one of suspension. Only the method of composing with twelve notes 'which are related only with one another', as Schoenberg significantly called the twelve-note principle, permitted the musical symbolization of eternity and God's infinity.

The eternal will summons Moses with the words 'Here lay the shoes aside. You stand on ground that is holy. Be God's prophet!' Moses bends to the eternal will with the words 'Only one, infinite, thou omnipresent one, unperceived and inconceivable God!' This, then, is why the theme already appears with this prayer (bars 8–10): perception and fulfilment of the eternal will are for Moses the idea, the law.

God as the infinite, as *ens*: and God as the idea to be realized by mankind—these are the two central concepts, and as such, they are embodied in two musical symbols; there the chords, here the theme. The action of the opera is the fate of these two concepts, and this fate is symbolically reflected in the musical transformations to which chords and theme are subjected.

Let us first trace the fate of the theme.

In the scene of Moses' calling, of the revelation and annunciation of God's will, the theme remains symbolically in equilibrium. The rhythmic and dynamic changes to which it is subjected do not alter its character. One of the principal means of later variation, the transposition of single notes to other octaves, is still almost entirely absent here, except in such passages as bars 3 and 5, where the steep ascent of the theme through several octaves is a telling gesture. In all the other passages listed below, the theme remains musically unchanged; its symbolic meaning does not alter.

Act I, Scene 1: bars 3, 5, 8–10, 11–15, 17, 18, 23, 24, 25, 26–27, 34, 44, 48–50, 67–68, 69–70, 79–80, 85.

Since, at the beginning of the second scene, Aaron's soul is wholly inhabited by the will of God, the theme is worked here into his vocal line ('on our brothers the infinite's grace', bars 136–138, and 'to belong to God . . .', bars 141–142). It dominates Aaron's recitative, where it is again placed in the vocal line ('Invisible! Inconceivable!' bars 178–185; simultaneously in the first horn, bars 183–186). During Aaron's emotional outburst towards the end of the scene, however, the theme does not occur at all.

In the crowd-scene (Act I, Scene 3), before the entry of Moses and Aaron, the theme is worked directly into the choral parts, but in a manner scarcely noticeable to the listener, serving as a psychological reflection of the various reactions of the people to the name of Moses: I, bars 296–297 ('He fled! We then suffered the wrath') and bars 299–300 ('Does he return to stir up rebellion?').

After the entry of Moses and Aaron, the dramatic action of the remainder of the scene, to the end of the act, consists of five phases:

1. Moses and Aaron announce to the people that they have been chosen by God (bars 480–490).
2. The people's defiance (bars 491–522).
3. Aaron, alone, addresses the people. Renewed defiance of the people (bars 523–620).
4. Moses at the end of his strength (bars 621–628).
5. Aaron works miracles (bars 630–916):
   (a) rod—snake (bars 642–673): first positive reaction of the people (bars 684–706);
   (b) Moses' hand—leprosy (bars 737–783): second reaction (bars 794–831);
   (c) water—blood (bars 868–916): third reaction (bars 918 to end).

In this dramatic context, our theme and the forms derived from it gain new significance. In detail:

The theme occurs in the first horn, and in the vocal line (bars 481–482 and 489); the chords, too, are formed out of the series. All this is a parallel passage to bars 178–180, 183–186, of the same act.

At the words 'To worship?', the theme is split into two groups, consisting of the first three and the last three notes respectively.

Aaron's words are based on the theme (bars 523–526, 530–533, 547–550).

Bars 623–628 are the parallel passage to bars 48–53 of the same act.

Bars 642–644 (Aaron: 'This rod leads you'); bars 788–790 (People: 'The hand is now hale and strong!'); bars 856–867 (Moses: 'In the wasteland, pureness of thought will provide you nurture'); bar 860; bar 861; bars 861–862; bars 866–867 four times, twice each in the principal and subordinate parts (Aaron: 'He who changed rod to serpent, and health to leprosy'); bar 868 (first and second crotchet in the orchestra); bars 893–895 (Aaron: 'But the almighty one will free you and free your blood'); bars 906–907 (in the orchestra, to Aaron's words: 'This is his promise'; parallel passage to bars 79–80 of the first act); bars 912–914, twice in the orchestra (Aaron: '. . . in spirit was vowed to your fathers'); bar 916 (orchestra); bars 927–928 in the orchestra (parallel passage to I, bars 79–80, 906–907).

A few passages may now be quoted in full; they show variants of the theme created by Schoenberg to meet the need of symbolic representation. When Aaron changes the water to blood, a distorted image of the original thematic form appears in the orchestra (Ex. 11):

Example 11 (*I, bar* 868)

Aaron's miracles are feats of sorcery. Complementary to this passage is bar 916 (Ex. 12):

Example 12 (*I, bar* 916)

after Aaron's words, 'What for Pharaoh remains, look here, is once more the Nile's clear water.'

In the second act, during the drift from God and the denial of God's will, the theme is hardly used. It appears in the first scene (II, bars 60 and 61) to the words of the priest: 'Unperceivable command from the unperceivable God'; in accordance with these words, it is a musical enigma: two chord-columns, each of nine notes, that twice include the theme (Ex. 13):

Example 13 (*II, bars* 60–61)

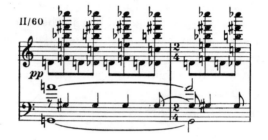

In the third scene, the lowest point in the denial of God is reached. The theme is rhythmically distorted (Ex. 5).

During these orgies of idolatry, the youth enters, trying to win back the people to the right faith: 'As high as thought were we once upraised, far from the present, close to the future!' (Ex. 14).

Example 14 (*II, bars* 560–565)

('As high as thought were we once upraised, present afar, future at hand!')

Motive *c* of his song is the symbol of God's will.

Moses returns from the sacred mountain and sees the Golden Calf. Terror, indignation and holy wrath seize him. The notes of the theme of God's will are torn far apart (Ex. 15):

Example 15 (*II, bars* 975–977)

In the dialogue between the two brothers, the theme gains a new, and enhanced, significance:

Act II, bar 990 ('Nevertheless, I still comprehended', two dovetailed statements of the theme); bars 1003–1005 ('These are the commands . . .', twice); bars 1050–1051 ('. . . you will then find your people . . .'); bars 1052–1053 ('I do not wish to see it!'); bar 1059 (the breaking of the tables of the law, Ex. 16); bars 1092–1093 ('God-sent signal . . .'); bars 1095–1096 ('but shows the way . . .'); bar 1099 (twice); bars 1110–1113 ('Inconceivable God!', Ex. 45); bars 1116–1118 ('. . . will you let it be so explained?', Ex. 45).

The fate to which the divine will is subjected by the agency of man is thus expressed through the fate of a theme. Two further passages may be quoted: the breaking of the Tables (Ex. 16, theme: F sharp, G, F, B, C sharp, C), and the last return of the

Example 16 (*II, bar* 1059)

theme, to Moses's words 'Inconceivable God! Inexpressible, many-sided idea, will you let it be so explained?' Here, the theme is transformed almost beyond recognition (Ex. 17, cf. also Ex. 45):

Example 17 (*II, bars* 1110–1118)

Strictly in accordance with a principle of compositional technique first used by Haydn, two motives are drawn from the theme and given autonomous stature: the first three notes ((*a*) of Ex. 10), forming a semitone–wholetone progression (see also Ex. 18), and notes 4–6 (b), forming a wholetone–semitone progression (see also Ex. 19). This musical process is also closely related to the symbolism of the work. At the end of the first scene, the voice

from the Burning Bush calls to Moses, 'Go forth now!' (Ex. 18
and 19):

Example 18 (*I, bars* 91–92)

Example 19 (*I, bar* 94)

('Go forth now!')

Schoenberg's artistic imagination creates an infinite variety of
contexts in which these three notes—according to their symbolic
significance—are transformed by rhythmic or dynamic changes,
by octave transposition and re-orchestration. A few examples may
be singled out:

At first, Moses proves weak in the sight of God's will ('I can
think, but not speak', Act I, Scene 1, Ex. 20):

Example 20 (*I, bars* 51–52)

The monumental, archaic, unison songs of the seventy elders in
the second act are almost exclusively based on motives (a) and
(b); as, for instance, in Ex. 21:

Example 21 (*II, bars* 77–82)

Vier - zig Ta - ge war-ten wir ver - ge-bens vor die-ser Hö - - he!

('Forty days now we have waited vainly before this summit!')

The thematic material of the 'scherzo' of the symphony, 'The Golden Calf and the Altar', is derived largely from these two motives. The 'swaying dance tempo' begins with the motive simultaneously in the upper and lower lines (Ex. 22):

Example 22 (*II, bars* 605–610)

The rhythmic turbulence of the symphony's third movement is further enhanced by the monotony of the motive. At a much broader speed, the Ephraimite sings Ex. 23:

Example 23 (*II, bars* 526–537)

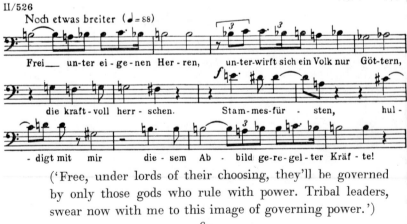

Frei__ un-ter ei - ge-nen Her - ren, un-ter-wirft sich ein Volk nur Göt-tern,

die kraft-voll herr - schen. Stam-mes-für - sten, hul -

- digt mit mir die - sem Ab - bild ge-re-gel-ter Kräf - te!

('Free, under lords of their choosing, they'll be governed by only those gods who rule with power. Tribal leaders, swear now with me to this image of governing power.')

The same motives dominate the orgiastic final movement (II, bars 824–966, see Ex. 7), where they represent, musically and symbolically, the opposite of their original meaning.

Finally, a quotation from the last scene (Moses calls Aaron to account, Aaron timidly gropes for excuses) which may, at the same time, serve as an example of the germinative power of this motive within the musical texture. The theme of the divine will appears in the first and second crotchet of bar 991, first in the bass, and then continuing in the upper part (Ex. 24):

Example 24 (*II, bars* 991–992)

('Cease!' 'Your . . . mouth . . .')

New musical cells are created by the juxtaposition and integration of the intervallic steps, as in the scene of the Burning Bush (Ex. 25):

Example 25 (*I, bars* 44–45)

('And by your rod, then by your hand!')

65

E

The musical representation of the rod is a succession of four semitone steps (I, bars 642–644).When Aaron defends himself, and particularly at his words 'Unbeknown, what you want will be done', motives consisting of semitone steps are linked to one another (II, bars 1043–1049).

VII

God the Infinite

Higher than the divine will and its symbol is eternal being, the infinity of God, expressed musically by the four chords quoted above (Ex. 9). When God speaks to Moses from the Burning Bush, these chords are already subjected to the articulation of language (I, bars 11–15, 23–24, 36–40, 59–60, 86–87).

As has already been pointed out, the four chords are never again stated with the perfect symmetry that they have in the first three bars of the opera. All later recurrences are only transformations, symbolic modifications; the eternal being of God manifests itself in finiteness.

In the following instances, the chords still retain their majesty, solemnity and stature: they dominate, in broad *sostenuto*, the last bars of the first scene; in low position, they are heard mysteriously in the orchestra as Aaron seizes upon the idea of God (I, bars 178–180); they form the quiet end of the second scene (I, bars 241–243); in the fourth scene, the six solo voices call 'Aaron!' (I, bars 630–631) and 'See!' (I, bar 780). But even in these passages, the dichotomy is already noticeable: the symmetry is abolished. The division of the four chords into groups of two, the quotation of one chord only, the adding of notes that do not belong to the original shape of the chords and its symbolism—these are objectivizations of the pure idea. After all, what Moses is commanded to convey to his brother or the people is pronounced by a human mouth, which can be no more than a mediator and means of proclamation. The recognition of the pure idea by human imagination signifies a diminution, a darkening; and this diminution eventually turns into denial and betrayal.

Only if we assume this theological viewpoint are we able to pursue the transmutations—musically speaking, variations—undergone musically and symbolically by these chords.

The first step in the symbolic and musical metamorphosis is the division of the four-chord unit into two chords; the next, the isolation of a single chord. The following examples are cases in point.

During the brothers' encounter in the desert, Aaron sings, 'People chosen by the only one' (I, bar 179, Ex. 26):

Example 26 (*I, bar* 179)

('People chosen by the only one, can you worship . . .')

Here, the two chords follow each other solemnly at slow speed, and Aaron meditatively sings his words to the theme of the divine will. Compare this with Ex. 11: the same theme appears distorted in the orchestra, the bass supplying a grotesque version of the divine idea. Yet it is the same Aaron who is at work.

Now an example from the second stage of isolation. The tribal leaders, in the fanaticism of their heathen ways, slay the youth. Three bars of music accompany the murderous deed. Let us single out the last bar (Ex. 27):

Example 27 (*II, bar* 594)

In the bass, the notes F sharp–A flat–G, the symbol 'Proclaim!';
on the third and fourth crotchets the same symbol, on the notes
C–B flat–B; in between, as quaver syncopations, the two chords,
torn asunder, isolated, acute: a last cry of death. This is music
which, even in a mood of extreme realism, does not renounce
its allegiance to spirituality.

Further steps towards isolation even transform the chord itself.
It is possible within the framework of twelve-note composition
to exchange the notes of a sound-combination. Thus, new musical
combinations come into being, which are again at the service of
symbolism.

Finally, the possibilities of transformation become limitless as
soon as further, foreign notes are added to the three notes of the
chord. 'Aaron shall be your mouth', the voice calls from the
Burning Bush (Ex. 28).

Example 28 (*I, bars* 59–61)

('Aaron shall be your mouth!')

With the words 'Aaron shall be', the chord occurs twice, super-
imposed upon itself, to form a six-part combination. At the words
'be your mouth', a symbolic change occurs which diminishes
the purity of the idea: though the second chord is preserved in
the notes F–A flat–E, its meaning is blunted by the notes
A–G flat–G. The identical juxtaposition of chords, exact even as
to pitch, recurs in the fourth scene (I, bars 630–631), when the
six solo voices call 'Aaron!'

At the beginning of the opera, the chords extend across the
interval of the major seventh, while the melody in the upper
part moves in major seconds. The last possible reduction of the

symbol is therefore the major seventh as a vertical interval, and the major second as a melodic step. The major seventh is frequently used to represent the chord; the interval of a second is particularly important in the opening scene.

VIII

God's Promise

In the promise to the Jewish people, God's will becomes concrete as an idea that is to be realized in the life of men. Moses is the proclaimer, the medium of the thought (Ex. 10); it is his task to awaken the idea in the people so that the promise may be fulfilled. This is why the promise is clothed in two new themes (Ex. 25 and 30), divided into two parts, in correspondence with the text, and arranged musically in two large movements:

Example 29 (*I, bars* 71–74)

('Your people are the chosen ones. They are the people of the one God')

Example 30 (*I, bars* 81–85)

('I shall conduct you forward, to where with the infinite oneness you'll be a model to every nation')

Musically, it is possible to consider the two new thoughts as a formal development of the themes of God's will: (b) and (c) encompass the first four notes of the theme, (a) the last four; (b) is the retrograde of (a); (c) is the inversion of (b), and identical with the retrograde inversion of (a). Motive (d), the symbol of 'Proclaim!' (Ex. 18 and 19) occurs eight times, with several overlaps. The four-note motive (e) is new, and new also are the intervals of the minor third, and the major sixth ('this people').

Is it accidental that the notes of 'you'll be a model'[1] in the soprano are the retrograde of the great name-symbol B–A–C–H?[2] The alto brings to the same words the name itself: Es[3] (Sebastian) B–A–C–H–.

Throughout the opera, the major sixth symbolizes the people of Israel; the people, that is, who are chosen by God. In the second act (II, bar 135), Aaron begins his pacifying address (Ex. 31):

Example 31 (II, bar 135)

Aaron still tries to mediate (vacillation between major and minor sixth). His second address (II, bars 173–174) begins with the same words; but now he is giving back to the people their heathen gods (Ex. 32):

Example 32 (bars 173–174)

In the songs of jubilation ('Joyous Israel!') which precede the worship of the Golden Calf, the sixth is no longer to be found;

[1] The notes referred to here coincide with the words 'every nation' of the English version.
[2] In English notation, this of course becomes B flat – A – C – B.
[3] E flat.

it recurs, however, in the symphonic pieces of the third scene, but now distorted (Ex. 2, 3, 4, 6, 8).

During his self-justification, Aaron speaks to his brother of

Example 33 (II, bar 989)

Ich hör-te die Stimme in mir,

('I heeded the voice from within')

his inner voice (Ex. 33), and identifies himself with the people (Ex. 34):

Example 34 (II, bars 1015–1019)

Ich lie - be die - ses Volk, — ich le - be für

es — und will es er - hal - ten!

('I love this humble people. I live just for them and want to sustain them')

When Moses smashes the Tables, Aaron remonstrates with him (Ex. 35):

Example 35 (II, bar 1060)

Klein-mü - ti-ger!

('Faint-hearted one!')

With the words 'Faint-hearted one!' we find the major sixth and the minor second (derived from 'this people').

73

The great hymn of the people has a song-like construction and begins each time (four times in all) with Ex. 36, which concludes with the major sixth.

Example 36 (I, bars 936–939)

('Almighty, thou art stronger than Egyptian gods are')

The sixth appears as an interval for the first time in the first scene (bar 16) to Moses's words 'God of my fathers', and is specially marked by Schoenberg as the principal part. If, throughout the work, one relates the use of the major sixth and the minor sixth to the meaning of the text, one comes to the conclusion that the major sixth is characteristic of God's promise to the people, while the minor sixth a kind of inflection of it, and as such specially characteristic of Aaron, with his exuberance, his emphatic intensity and his thinking in images. Already in the second scene (bar 148), he speaks of God as 'vision of highest fantasy': *he* makes an image of God, while for Moses, God is the law (Ex. 37):

Example 37 (bars 148–152)

('O vision of highest fantasy, how glad it is that you've enticed it to form you')

Image and prudence are synonyms for Aaron (Ex. 38):

Example 38 (*I, bars* 660–661)

('Discretion!')

To quote two other passages from his address to the people (Ex. 39 and 40):

Example 39 (*II, bars* 308–309)

('This gold image attests . . .')

Example 40 (*II, bars* 312–313)

('The gold that you have given')

The chords that symbolize God's infinity (Ex. 9), and the theme that symbolizes God's will (Ex. 10) are complemented by the symbol of the promise (Ex. 29 and 30), the third of the great spiritual concepts of the work. The various restatements, and their significance within the action, have been discussed above. Let us, however, look once more at the beginning of the hymn (Ex. 36). The verse-line begins with the motive (a) of God's promise (Ex. 29) and is continued by the retrograde form of motive (b) (Ex. 30).

The themes of promise, and their constituents, pervade the music of the entire work. Without aiming at completeness, I should like to indicate some of the crucial points at which the themes (a) and (b) are interpolated.

When the two brothers meet in the desert, Aaron greets Moses ('O son of my fathers . . . ') with the theme of promise (I, bars 124–126, 130–132). At his words 'O happy people to have one mighty god to belong to . . .' (bars 139–145) we find in the vocal part, in close juxtaposition, Ex. 30 (e) (retrograde), then Ex. 10, and dovetailed with it Ex. 30 (b). Moses's summons to his brother—the only passage which may be sung by Moses—uses Ex. 29 (a) and 30 (e) (bars 208–214); the same passage is repeated by the orchestra at the end of the scene (bars 234–239).

In the great polyphonic choruses of the crowd, one of the themes is Ex. 30 (b) (Ex. 41):

Example 41 (*I, bars* 335–336)

('The newest god also will not help us!')

As already mentioned, the beginning of the hymn is derived from Ex. 29 (a), (b) and (c) (I, bars 689–691, 798–800, 936–938; II, bars 1101–1109).

When Aaron sings 'The all-knowing one knows that you are still a childlike people . . .', he uses the themes of Ex. 29 (a) and Ex. 10, adjacently (bars 845–847). He unfolds the entire promise, which is then repeated by the people (bars 897–912, 918–933).

In the double-fugue of the Interlude, the first fugue-subject is derived from Ex. 29 (a), 30 (b) and 10:

Example 42 (*Interlude, bars* 5–8)

('Ne'er, ne'er, ne'er, shall we see him! Where is he?')

The fanfares that introduce the sacrifices and the arrival of the tribal leaders (Ex. 1), derive from Ex. 29 (a) (II, bars 320–

327 and 497–501). The pointed, rhythmic march-theme (Ex.
6, bars 502–504 *inter alia*) is a variant of Ex. 29 (a). The frenzied
song of the zealous youth includes Ex. 30 (e) (bars 560–561,
564–565, 566, 571, cf. Ex. 14), as well as Ex. 29 (a) in bars
574–578. The climax of the orgy, the fifth movement of the
symphony, begins with Ex. 29 (a), completely distorted (Ex.
7, bar 828); then, in bar 831 we have the theme of Ex. 10, but
only in part and caricatured, as also in bar 833; then Ex. 29 (a)
again, in bars 834–835.

Aaron defends himself before his brother, in diabolical
fashion, by trying to convince him of the genuineness of images:
here, Ex. 29 (a) and 30 (b) are time and again woven into his
vocal line (bars 999, 1000, 1036–1039, 1043, 1047–1048, 1055,
1062–1063).

The columns of fire and cloud appear in the sky; the people,
driven to fanaticism once more, intone the statement of the
promise. Aaron, convinced of the divine power of his magic,
leads the singing; this is the rejoicing of a crowd that is still far
removed from Moses's insistence on the law and knowledge of
God. The march-rhythms in the orchestra, the themes (Ex. 6,
10, 18, 19) and the chords (Ex. 9)—all hectic shouts—indicate
that the people are dominated by demonic powers.

One may speak here of a polyphony of symbols; of the simul-
taneity and succession of the various themes that together con-
stitute the totality of a musical texture that possesses complete
autonomy of form. Counterpoint of this kind is found also in the
song of the youth that was quoted as Ex. 14 (II, bars 560–565).
Motives (a) and (b) correspond, (b) being the retrograde of (a):
this is the motive of divine ecstasy; (c) is Ex. 10, (d) is Ex. 30 (b),
(e) is Ex. 18 ('Proclaim!').

The symbol of divine ecstasy is included in the promise
('conduct you forward', I, bar 81, Ex. 30 (e)). Characteristic of
this motive in its original form is the succession of semitone-
minor third and semitone-wholetone steps (or vice versa in the
motive's retrograde form, as in Ex. 30 (e)). As early as the

second scene, this motive is interwoven, in various ways, into the vocal line and orchestral part of Aaron's dialogue with Moses (I, bars 127–128, 134, 139–140, 158–159, 161, 187, 212–213, 238–239).

It is not until the third scene, however, when the three followers of the new faith step before the people, that the theme acquires its ecstatic quality (Ex. 43):

Example 43 (I, bars 255–264)

('I saw him afar, just as a flame hotly glowing sprang forth and addressed him. He threw himself on his knees and concealed his face in the sand. He then went forth in the wasteland.')

Religious exultation and the expectation of freedom intermingle (Ex. 44):

Example 44 (I, bars 397–399)

('He shall make us free!')

Thus, the symbolic significance of the motive is enlarged, and in the further course of the work it assumes many forms.

In connection with the polyphony of symbols, the great unison line for the violins at the breakdown of Moses (bars 1108–1136. the final bars of the work) is one single spiritual-musical convolution of symbols, born of the utter despair of a man who has lost faith in his strength. Below, we quote the conclusion of the work, indicating the words of Moses and the orchestral accompaniment, but excluding the close of the march-like music from behind the stage, which ends at bar 1109, and the receding shouts of the people. On the third stave, the orchestral part is reduced to a medium range; the repeated notes are omitted and the rhythm ignored, so that the basic forms of the themes may be seen more easily.

Example 45 (*II, bars* 1108–1136)

die - se Aus-legung zu? Darf A - ron, mein Mund, dieses Bild ma-chen?

So ha - be ich mir ein Bild gemacht, falsch wie ein Bild nur

sein kann! So bin ich ge-schlagen! So war al - les

(So rasch als möglich von Note zu Note beschleunigen)

Wahn-sinn, was ich ge - dacht ha - be,

('Inconceivable God! Inexpressible, many-sided idea, will you let it be so explained? Shall Aaron, my mouth, fashion this image? Then I have fashioned an image, too, false, as an image must be. Thus am I defeated! Thus, all was but madness that I believed before, and can and must not be given voice. O word, thou word, that I lack!')

Bars 1108–1112 bring the inversion of 'The people of the one God alone' (Ex. 29). At bar 1110, the symbol of the law enters contrapuntally (Ex. 10), while dovetailed with this (bar 1113) is the motive of divine ecstasy (Ex. 43), whose fundamental significance is that of the promise ('I shall conduct you forward', Ex. 30). With the note F sharp of bar 1113, 'The people of one God alone' enters for the second time (bars 1113–1116); the theme of the law (bars 1116–1118) is woven in to create thematic polyphony. The beginning of the promise ('This people is chosen', Ex. 29) appears in retrograde motion from bar 1118 to

81

F

1123. The D sharp of bar 1120 is, as it were, the upbeat to the motive of religious ecstasy (Ex. 43) which is extended to bar 1125. In bar 1124, 'Go forth now!' enters (the notes G–A–B flat, to bar 1127). These two motives, the motive of religious ecstasy, and 'Go forth now!' are interwoven three times (D sharp–E–G–A and G–A–B flat) into the rushing semi-quaver figures of bar 1127. The last two notes of bar 1127 belong again to the symbol of divine will (Ex. 10). This is broken off on the low C of bar 1131 (we only hear notes 1–5 of the theme); in its place there appear, in bars 1131–1132, the notes 4–6 of the theme (A flat–D–C–B). The last seven notes of the composition (D–C–B–C sharp–F–F sharp, bars 1131–1136) are the words of the promise, 'I shall lead you forward' (I, bars 81 and 82, Ex. 30). The retrograde is here not only a purely musical device but a symbol in its own right. Allegorically, the retrograde motion anticipates the content of the third act: Moses again finds the strength for his task.

IX
Aaron: Eternal Change

W hich are the symbols that belong to Aaron? This question must now be faced. It is not the text, but the score, as the fulfilment of the poem, which gives us the key to Aaron's character as it was conceived by Schoenberg. Moses is a speaking role; the proclaimer of the idea, significantly, is denied song. Aaron, on the other hand, the exegesist, the rhetorician, the weaver of fantasies, is granted song, the medium of sensuality.

There are many moments in the score—they have already been described—when Aaron weaves into his song the themes and symbols that belong to God and his mandate to Moses, and are thus part of Moses's world; this happens whenever Aaron, unwittingly rather than deliberately, receives some intimation—grasps the shadow—of this world. But his proper realm is that of the image, of eternal change. And thus, both his song and his musical characterization by the orchestra are subject to perpetual change.

Twice only does he have a theme of his own. 'He floated rather than walked; hardly indeed did he touch the ground', is said of him as, following God's summons, he hastens to the desert. This is depicted in the music of the prelude to the second scene: the flute plays a theme that extends across twenty-six bars, that continually renews itself, as it were, out of itself (Ex. 46). This theme also appears at the beginning of the brothers' discussion (to bar 147); and brief, occasional references are subsequently made to it (I, bars 487–488, 838–845; also II, bars 1023–1028, 1043–1047); at these moments the political realist seems to be inspired by enthusiasm for some higher ideal.

Example 46 (I, bars 98–105)

One of Aaron's character-traits is the love for his people with which he is filled, and which gives to his song the semblance of a hymn (Ex. 47):

Example 47 (I, bars 163–176)

('Chosen is this people, thus to love one great god for ever and ever, with a thousand times more devotion than all other earthly peoples for their many godly beings.')

Quoted literally, or in some form of derivation, this theme, too, returns several times (in I, bar 186, and subsequently in the orchestra; also bar 218 *et seq.*; and in II, bar 1015, and then in the orchestra). In all other contexts, Aaron's musical characterization is that of a sorcerer, an artist of transmutation, a seducer and demon, equivocal, restless, carrying good and evil within himself, but effecting evil, destruction. He is a man without the life of the spirit. In him, Schoenberg has created a figure that can take its rightful place with similar figures in world literature.

X

Music, Language
and Symbols

Is the discovery of symbols the one and only approach to the work?

This question coincides with the consideration whether or not the spiritual and thematic symbols that have already been elucidated are successfully active and effective in every passage of the work, down to the smallest phrase or subsidiary counterpoint.

Systematization was foreign to Schoenberg, to both the man and the artist, throughout his life. The symbolic web is no more the only form-giving agency of the music than it is with Bach.

We have noted above that, formally, the music contains both closed and free sections. The extremes of formal contrast are reached wherever a kind of musical prose, on the one hand, and polyphonic structure, on the other, confront each other.

The treatment of the vocal parts is conditioned by the spirit of language, that is, of the German language. Thus Schoenberg takes his place in a tradition that has always been particularly prominent whenever the spirit has triumphed over the sensual element of music, and over musical form. The works of Schütz, Bach, Mozart (*The Magic Flute*) and Wagner are outstanding landmarks in the history of word-setting created out of the spirit of the German language. We are speaking here of the principle that Wagner called *Sprachgesang*: a translation of the spoken word into the acoustic realm, a 'carrying-across' in the literal meaning of the Latin word *translatio*; a process that produces values of which the spoken word itself is not capable. This not only means that words and sentences, as conveyors of meaning, are raised to the status of elevated prose, but that their content of ideas, their spiritual aura, is encompassed and expressed by music. It is from this that all the various nuances in the differentiation of note-progressions and their dynamic and rhythmic gradings are derived. The same principle applies to the sung parts, as well as to the speaking role of Moses, and also to the choruses, which partly sing, partly speak. For speech too, has a musical function; though pitch is only approximate, and any suggestion of singing must be avoided, its rhythm is strictly defined. An approach to language as brilliantly resourceful as this is in no danger of slavish subjection to musical symbols and laws: the latter will, on the contrary, be used freely as a function of sovereign diction.

And so the treatment of language takes its place beside musical symbolism, with its spiritual message. The third factor, however, is a purely musical one: the laws of melody and part-writing. It is true, of course, that all the musical symbols described above are subject to the purely musical laws of melodic formulation; after all, they are the fruits of musical imagination and not the constructions of musical rationality. Yet when Schoenberg states the two great ideas of the promise as a *cantus firmus*, first in the alto, then in the alto and tenor, then in the soprano, while building around this, with the co-operation of all the voices, a great six-part polyphonic movement that is further augmented by the orchestra—then it is the finely conceived laws of polyphony, part-writing and melody that make their autonomous claims, and, in the event, govern the structure. The symbol-carrying theme stands by itself as a *cantus firmus*, the other parts are functional aspects of the musical structure. The same is true of the great polyphonic choruses, whose *dramatic* impact is of purely musical origin; their *spiritual* power is derived from the interrelation of the principal themes within the symbolic web. From these three principles—the themes as symbols, musical prose, and melodic-polyphonic laws of form—the totality of the work of art is seamlessly woven.

In considering the symbolism of musical themes and their

recurrence, we must not think of Wagner's *Leitmotiv* technique. The musical symbols in Schoenberg's opera, and Wagner's lead-ing-motives, merely rest on a common basis: the ability of music to act as the expressive form (symbol) of a given conceptual and affec-tive content. Certain contents and musical themes present themselves simultaneously, and blend, in a new unity, in the listener's mind. With Wagner, the themes themselves are symbols for ideas, objects, external events, sentiments or dramatic impulses.

A few examples will suffice. The treaty which Wotan makes with the giants in *Das Rheingold* is symbolized by a theme that is musically derived from another theme, the 'spear-motive'; a symbol for a real, visible object, the spear. The 'riding-motive' characterizes an external event of the action; the love-motives from the first act of *Die Walküre* symbolize sentiments and emotions.

With Schoenberg, on the other hand, there is only *one* spiritual idea. Its name is God; and it is in the summons to Moses, and the promise to the people, that this idea manifests itself. It is the focus of the work, and not a *Leitmotiv*, either in its spiritual or in its musical significance; it is the life of the spirit itself. If there is any parallel in music that could be compared with Schoenberg's central world of spiritual symbols, it is to be found in Bach's sacred vocal music. Here, too, the most disparate elements—themes, motives, harmonies, rhythms—have the function of symbols. They, too, have order: namely, in the hierarchy of the religious and spiritual world in which Bach believed and lived, thought and created.

Admittedly, Wagner also employs themes to symbolize salient spiritual ideas or spiritual powers; in the *Ring*, the 'curse-motive'; the syncopated figure ('destructive work of the Nibe-lungs'); the 'motive of the question to fate' (Schicksalsfrage); or the 'motive of world-inheritance'. In taking over the names of these motives from Hans von Wolzogen, it is well to remember that Wolzogen himself, in his guide to Wagner's *Ring* (Leip-zig, 1911) draws emphatic attention to the 'affective element' which is 'the true fundamental principle of all motive-formation'. This statement in itself provides us with a useful distinction between the motives in Wagner and the three central ideas in *Moses and Aaron*, the point being that the latter are *not* of affective origin. In the course of the dramatic action, to be sure, they are brought into affective relation; this occurs as a result of affectively determined factors in the plot, such as Moses's doubt of his own strength and anger at the people's desertion, Aaron's magic, the people's wavering and inconsistency. At this point, there emerges a second distinctive element of a purely musical nature. Wagner develops his motives according to classical principles of variation. Admittedly, these transformations are closely wedded to the meaning and the progress of dramatic events on the stage; yet in their changing forms and shapes they are purely musical variations.

Thematic variations do not occur in Schoenberg's opera; instead, we have the inexhaustible possibilities of variation which Schoenberg had opened up for himself through his commitment to the technique of twelve-note music. We shall say more about this technique later. The present analysis and interpretation may already have shown that, in *Moses and Aaron*, this technique is by no means used as a compositional device for its own sake, but exclusively in the service of the work's spiritual ideas. Seen from this angle, it becomes evident that, even on a purely musical level, the themes in Schoenberg's opera cannot be compared with Wagner's motives.

As musical symbols, Schoenberg's themes are in close, reciprocal rapport with the conceptual world that they symbolize; yet, at the same time, they are conceived as musical material capable of forming the basis of the subsequent variants.

It seems, moreover, that some mystical number-symbolism is at the back of Schoenberg's music, as it is of Bach's: the suggestion is made for what it is worth, in the absence of special studies on the subject. The number six seems to predominate: twelve notes are contained in the first four chords, each having three notes—the symbol of God's infiniteness. Six notes, twice three, are contained in the symbols of divine will. Six solo voices form the (sung) voice of God; a six-part speaking chorus forms the voice from the Burning Bush that conveys the biddings of the divine will.

Did Schoenberg ever come across the musicological studies of Schweitzer or Schering, in which the musical-spiritual relations of symbols were first elucidated? He surely recognized intuitively relations of this kind in Bach's music; their detailed, scientific investigation cannot have been the concern of the creative artist. The question is of no consequence, for Schoenberg had spiritual order within himself. Like Bach, two hundred years before him, he consummated the *unio mystica*, which alone is reflected in his music. Among the personal effects of Schoenberg, Josef Rufer found the great Bach Edition with numerous analytical glosses in each single volume. In a document entitled *National Music*, written in February, 1931, at the time of the conception of *Moses and Aaron*, Schoenberg wrote: 'My masters were in the first place Bach and Mozart; in the second, Beethoven, Brahms and Wagner. From Bach I have learnt (1) contrapuntal thinking; that is, the art of inventing musical shapes that are capable of being their own accompaniment; (2) the art of producing the all out of the one, and of leading from one texture to the next; (3) independence from the beat.' Schoenberg goes on to specify the stimuli he received; among other things, he claims to have learnt from Beethoven '(1) the art of developing themes and movements; (2) the art of variation and variant'; and from Wagner 'the mutability of a theme's expressive content, and how to invent themes with a view to this end'. Schoenberg, however, does not deal in this context with the art of setting words to music.

XI

The Third Act

Why did the third act, a single great scene, remain without music? Why did Schoenberg not continue, and work out the sketches he had put down for the music of the third act?

Let us try to find an answer on the basis of the recently published collection of Arnold Schoenberg's letters, and of the quotations from letters given by Gertrud Schoenberg in the published scores (vocal and orchestral) of the opera.

The following refer directly to our question:

'I would very much like to complete the opera before coming to Berlin.' (1931)

'I would like to finish the third act of my opera *Moses and Aaron*.' (1932)

'I intend to complete the third act the moment I go on leave —in six to eight weeks at the latest.' (1933)

'If I could work I should like best to finish *Die Jakobsleiter* and *Moses and Aaron*.' (1948) —

'I have already a very good idea of the music of the third act, and I believe I could write it in a few months . . .' (1949)

'. . . but have since found neither time nor inclination for the composition of the third act. As a matter of fact, the third act consists of one single scene only. . . . Everything depends on my nervous eye-ailment.' (1950)

'It is not quite impossible that I shall complete the third act within a year.' (1950)

'I agree that the third act may be performed as a spoken drama, without music, in case I should not be able to complete the composition.' (1951)

The work in the form we have it today, with the setting of the first two acts concluded, is complete. It is a whole. He who has experienced the *unio mystica* in which the opera was conceived and gestated, knows that it would have been completed if only the external circumstances of the 1930s and, later, the composer's precarious health, had permitted it. 'It suffices to understand and experience the work in its present form. As it is, so was it to be', Gertrud Schoenberg writes in the epilogue to the vocal score published in 1957. The various remarks contained in Schoenberg's letters leave no room for doubt that he was firmly resolved to complete the work's composition.

XII

The Twelve-note Character of the Music

Schoenberg always passionately opposed any view of his works that approached them exclusively from the angle of twelve-note technique. 'I cannot say it often enough: my works are twelve-note *compositions*, not *twelve-note* compositions.' Exclusive concern with twelve-note technique was energetically countered by him: '. . . it is not from this angle, or if at all only accidentally, that the aesthetic qualities reveal themselves. I cannot often enough warn against the overrating of analysis [implied is serial analysis] since it invariably leads to what I have always fought against: the knowledge of how something is *made*; whereas I have always tried to promote the knowledge of what something *is*! . . . To my mind, only that analysis is worthy of its name which emphasizes the idea and shows the latter's presentation and treatment. To be sure, felicities of craftsmanship must not be overlooked here either.'

Yet another quotation from Schoenberg may be apposite: 'The first idea of a row occurs always in the form of a thematic character.' Thus Schoenberg tells us that, for him, the creative idea is the starting-point of the compositional process. Creative imagination has absolute priority; it always comes before deliberate workmanship. The series is derived *a posteriori* from the themes, not the themes from the series. The series therefore is an abstraction, not the 'idea' of the work.

Schoenberg, then, did not base the composition of *Moses and Aaron* on a twelve-note series, but, on the contrary, abstracted the series from the themes. It is our task to find the connection

between the themes and the notes of the series. This is the series
(Ex. 48):

Example 48

But first of all, a brief reminder of the principles of twelve-
note composition.

The above-quoted form of the series is the *basic set*. According
to the principles of traditional counterpoint, one can derive from
the basic set the *inversion* (Ex. 49):

Example 49

Further, the *retrograde* (cancrizans) *motion* (Ex. 50):

Example 50

and, finally, the *retrograde of the inversion* (Ex. 51):

Example 51

Each of the four forms can be transposed to any of the twelve
degrees of the octave, so there are 48 possibilities. The position
of any note within the twelve notes of the octave is determined
by its place in the series. Not so its individual placing within
tonal space; i.e., each single note may appear within the range
of any octave. Equally, an immediate repetition of a note is
permitted. Since, furthermore, the rhythmic combinations in
which the notes may be grouped, are unlimited, the number of
possibilities becomes well-nigh inexhaustible. The 48 basic
positions are illustrated in the following table. From left to right,

with arabic numbers, we find the twelve transpositions of the basic set; from top to bottom, with roman numbers, the inversions of the basic set. Horizontally, reading from right to left, we find the twelve transpositions of the retrograde; vertically, reading from the bottom upwards, the twelve forms of the retrograde inversion.

	I	II	III	IV	V	VI	VII	VIII	IX	X	XI	XII
			→Basic Set									
1	A	Bb	E	D	Eb	Db	G	F	F#	G#	B	C
2	G#	A	Eb	C#	D	C	Gb	E	F	G	Bb	B
3	D	Eb	A	G	Ab	Gb	C	Bb	B	C#	E	F
4	E	F	B	A	Bb	Ab	D	C	C#	D#	F#	G
5	D#	E	Bb	G#	A	G	C#	B	C	D	F	F#
6	F	Gb	C	Bb	B	A	Eb	C#	D	E	G	Ab
7	B	C	F#	E	F	Eb	A	G	Ab	Bb	C#	D
8	C#	D	Ab	F#	G	F	B	A	Bb	C	D#	E
9	C	Db	G	F	F#	E	Bb	Ab	A	B	D	Eb
10	Bb	B	F	D#	E	D	Ab	F#	G	A	C	Db
11	G	Ab	D	C	C#	B	F	Eb	E	F#	A	Bb
12	F#	G	Db	B	C	Bb	E	D	Eb	F	G#	A

Retrograde←

A theme may contain all twelve notes of the series or any group of them. The group may contain consecutive notes of the series or a freely combined selection.

The series can also be abstracted from the vertical dimension (harmony). A fundamental law of twelve-note music permits a horizontal theme made of successive notes to be stated vertically in simultaneous sound.

The opera *Moses and Aaron* opens with a sequence of four chords (Ex. 9). The first chord consists of the notes 2–3–1 of the A-series in its basic form; the second chord of the notes 12–10–11 of the A-series in its basic form; the third chord (in the manner of a mirror form) of the notes 2–3–1 of the inverted retrograde of the A-series; the fourth of the notes 12–10–11 of the inverted retrograde.

The musical symbol of divine will (Ex. 10) appears in the A-series as a succession of notes 4–9.

The themes of the promise are reflected serially as follows:

The first theme (Ex. 29) contains, in bar 71, notes 12–7 of the series (retrograde), while bar 72 is an appended extension. Bar 73 contains notes 1–6 of the series (basic form); bar 74 is again merely appended.

The second theme (Ex. 30), in its first bar (81), is identical with notes 6–1 of the inverted retrograde; in its second bar (82), with the notes 7–12 of the direct retrograde. Bar 83 brings notes 7–12 of the inverted retrograde in succession; bar 84, notes 7–12 of the basic set, and bar 85 notes 1–2 of the basic set.

Thus the twelve-note series is seen to be indissolubly united with the three central, spiritual-musical symbols: God as infinity, God as will (law), and God's promise. In the course of the opera, all the transformations of these three ideas give rise to significant musical variants (Ex. 1, 5, 6, 7, 8, 11, 12, 13, 14, 15, 16, 17, 18, 19, 20, 21, 22, 23, 24, 25, 26, 27, 28, 33, 35, 36, 41, 42, 43, 44, 45), which, in their turn, are directly related to the twelve-note series. The three great themes, God, Law (mission) and Promise, signify order in its absolute aspect, and the twelve-note series is the symbol of this order. One might even venture a generalization: the further the people recede from God, the more freely Schoenberg treats the connection between themes and basic set. That is to say, themes such as Ex. 2, 3, 4, 31, 32, 34 or 37 combine the notes of the series more or less freely; or to put it more precisely, the series is stated vertically (comprising both voice and orchestra). In this way, pseudo-tonal relations come into existence; the themes in Ex. 2, 3 or 4, for instance, could, by themselves, be thought to have a tonal centre. But this is only apparently so, for, even here, the dodecaphonic principle is not renounced. As we have seen, the twelve-note series of the opera is the symbol of divine, spiritual order. For Schoenberg, it is a means to an end, as the series itself remains, as it were, silent. It is, however, an all-embracing note-constellation in which the total conception of the opera, as though it were pure idea, is contained, enveloped and encompassed. In the outward world of sound, this spiritual idea is made manifest in the musical symbols. The series regulates the symbols, and, by its ubiquity, establishes relationships between them. This, indeed, is why it cannot 'materialize' itself as sound. The symbols do this for the series. These considerations may show just how profound and indispensable the philosophical aspect has become, as a key to the understanding of the inner motivation of Schoenberg's music and his concept of serial technique.

In this work, Schoenberg succeeded in giving new meaning to traditional musical symbols. Since the baroque age, the triad has signified divine harmony; but with Schoenberg it is the reverse: the intervals and sound-combinations that fall pleasingly on the ear belong to the sensuous world; they symbolize the falling-away from God. God in his infinity, on the other hand, is symbolized by sound-combinations which, according to traditional harmony, have to be considered as dissonances. But they are not dissonances. Schoenberg brought about a complete reversal of traditional relationships and their perception, by means of a new spiritual concept of music.

It will be one of the tasks of future Schoenberg research to furnish convincing proof that the linguistic symbolism in Schoenberg's music is a strictly organic, unified and consistent phenomenon. The linguistic devices may assume different guises in different stylistic periods; yet in essence they remain the same. In this context we might suggest some parallels with the succession of chords named by us the symbol of God's infinity (Ex. 9), that exist in other works of Schoenberg. The most striking example occurs in the music from Maeterlinck's poem *Herzgewächse*, Op. 20, for soprano, celesta, harmonium and harp, written in 1911: in the last bars, to the words 'zum Kristall dem blauen sendet sie ihr mystisches Gebet' ('to the blue crystal she offers her mystical prayer'), the chord progressions of Ex. 52 express the restful, relaxed, floating character of the passage.

Example 52

G

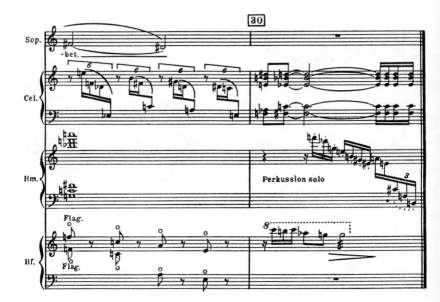

In *Erwartung*, composed in 1909, there is one single moment, at the beginning of the second scene, when the soul of the female protagonist is allowed to find inner peace. This is the passage in Marie Pappenheim's text:

(*Walks on, with outstretched arms*)
'The path is wide . . .'
(*Calmly reflecting*)
'It was so still behind the walls of the garden . . .'
(*Very quietly*)
'No scythes there . . . no calling and bustling, and the town in a radiant haze . . . longingly I looked across . . . and the sky so unfathomably deep above the path. . . .'

Example 53

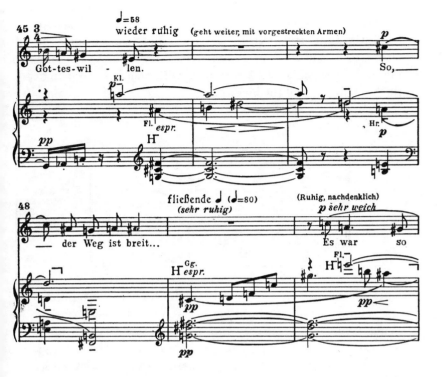

Musically, the whole section (see Ex. 53) is dominated by a calmly ascending melodic line which, on an ever-changing harmonic basis, recurs six times in all within twenty bars. The salient chord combinations here are augmented fourth plus perfect fourth, and augmented fifth plus minor third.

Schoenberg was no doubt aware of the organic unity and consistency of his creative work. This is confirmed by a passage from a letter of 1939: 'My music has never concerned itself with "style", but always with a content and its most precise presentation. This is why my early works prepare the listener for the understanding of my musical thoughts, and it is a good thing to become familiar with the former before tackling the later works, in which my mode of expression has become quite terse.'

99

In Schoenberg's string trio of 1946, the section entitled first episode, beginning at bar 52, is introduced by a melodic line comparable in structure (see Ex. 54). The emotional situation, too, is the same: the preceding climax, built on an accumulation of sighing accents, has now been succeeded by inner calm. Significantly, the entire work concludes with chords formed from the ascending line of the melody:

Example 54

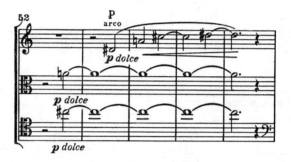

It will be another task for future research to establish, by means of tabulation, the incidence of certain well-defined vertical combinations in Schoenberg's music. It may then be recognized that the chords of Ex. 9 occur very frequently in Schoenberg's work. One may claim that they must, of necessity, play a significant role in the organization of non-tonal dodecaphonic music; for, apart from the combinations of two seconds, they are the only three-note chord combinations that do not immediately evoke tonal associations in a tonally conditioned ear. It is precisely by the inclusion of such fundamental issues in an analysis that deals with symbols and contents, that a more profound insight into the connections between musical logic and metaphysics and psychology can be achieved. In this context, the unmistakable connection that exists between the first three bars of the opera *Moses and Aaron* and the first three bars of the first piano piece of Op. 11 (1909) must be mentioned. Here, in Op. 11, is the gateway to non-tonal music; there, in the opera, non-tonal music is at its summit!

This exegesis does not aim to provide a twelve-note analysis of the opera *Moses and Aaron*. We should, however, like to draw the reader's attention to a few combinations which he may care to look up in the vocal or orchestral score, making use of the serial table given above.

Aaron's first words to his brother Moses (I, 2, bars 124–129) present the twelve-note basic set in the vocal line, beginning with C sharp (table, 8, left to right). At bar 130, Aaron's voice continues with the inversion of the basic set (beginning with E, III, top to bottom in the table, bars 130–134). There follows basic set 8, in retrograde (bars 135–138); then III (bars 139–145) as retrograde inversion.

Moses' words, 'Purify your thinking' (I, 2, bars 208–217), the only words in this role that 'may possibly be sung', use the twelve notes of the basic set in inversion, beginning with D (IV in the table, read from top to bottom).

The two themes of the Interlude's double-fugue are derived from the inversion of the basic set (I, read from top to bottom); the notes are distributed alternatively between the two themes.

The passionate monologue of the unison violins at the end of the second act uses, in its last section, the retrograde inversion of IX.

XIII
The Performances

On April 10, 1930, Schoenberg wrote to his friend Alban Berg from Baden-Baden, congratulating him on the success of his opera *Wozzeck*, and mentioning briefly his own recent works. He then goes on: 'What I'm going to write now, I don't know yet . . . perhaps I'll do *Moses and Aaron*.'

There is also a very interesting letter, written at Territet on August 8, 1931, again addressed to Alban Berg, who is being kept informed about the progress of Schoenberg's work on the opera, and who, as Schoenberg knows, is working at his own opera *Lulu*. Schoenberg says: 'It is only while I'm composing that the text becomes definite, sometimes even after composition. This, of course, is only possible if one has a very exact idea of everything, and the trick is not only to keep this vision continuously alive, but to strengthen, enrich and enlarge it while working out the details.' Now follows the sentence quoted above, from which it appears that Schoenberg wanted to finish the opera before his return to Berlin. 'I'm not getting on as quickly as I hoped at first, when I was reckoning with a daily average of twenty bars. I'm far behind my schedule. Main reason: the text and the choruses. The writing of the choral parts alone takes such a long time that even the working-out of a four-to six-part passage is a trifle by comparison. Besides, I'm delayed by the fact that I'm writing a complete score all at once, and that takes a lot of time. But, of course, there is the advantage that I'll have finished with everything the moment I have composed the last note.' Later, Schoenberg comments on the ability to return to a work after an interruption of several months, and to resume at the point where one stopped. 'I fear only one thing:

that I shall have forgotten everything I have written. For even now I'm hardly able to recognize what I wrote last year. And if it were not for some sort of unconscious memory that involuntarily puts me back on to the right musical and textual tracks, I should be at a loss to know how to give organic unity to the whole.'

And once again it is Alban Berg whom he informs about the progress of the work. On January 20, 1932, Berg is told, from Barcelona, that the text of the second act, which Berg had already read, had been revised 'several times over'. 'You would be surprised to see how far-reaching—though, to be sure, to the benefit of the work—the alterations are.'

Schoenberg's manuscript score bears on its first page the inscription 'Lugano, July 17, 1930'. At the end of the second act we find 'Barcelona, March 10, 1932'. The Interlude was begun on July 20, 1931, at Territet (Switzerland) and completed on the 25th. According to an entry in the score, the second act was begun on July 25, 1931. This manuscript score, in which the definitive wishes of the composer are embodied, was preceded by an autograph in the form of a sketch, in which the music is for the most part worked out bar by bar and notated, as the case may be, on one to seven staves; while some sections are worked out in great detail, others consist of the vocal line alone. As in the definitive score, this sketch, too, bears the entry 'Lugano, July 17, 1930'. The earliest sketch of the music, found among Schoenberg's legacy, is marked in Schoenberg's hand 'Berlin, May 7, 1930.'

On Monday, July 2, 1951, a special concert took place at Darmstadt, under the auspices of the International Summer Course for New Music, in which an excerpt from the opera, the *Dance round the Golden Calf*, was performed for the first time. The conductor was Hermann Scherchen, the soloists Ruth Wilke (soprano), Petra Boser (contralto), Franz Köth (tenor), Heinz Janssen (tenor) and Willibald Vohla (bass). The chorus of the Landestheater, Darmstadt, augmented by members of the local choral society, was trained by Paul Cadow. The work was played by the augmented orchestra of the Landestheater, Darmstadt.

The first complete concert performance was given by the Nordwestdeutscher Rundfunk, Hamburg, as part of its series of public performances devoted to new music, at the Hamburger Musikhalle, under the direction of Hans Rosbaud, on Friday, March 12, 1954. Those taking part were the united choirs of NWDR, Cologne (chorus-masters Bernhard Zimmermann and Otto Maier), of the NWDR Hamburg (chorus-masters Max Thurn and Otto Franze), and the Hamburger Statliche Hochschule für Musik (chorus-master Adolf Detel); the symphony orchestra of NWDR, Hamburg; Hans Herbert Fiedler (Moses), Helmut Krebs (Aaron), Ilona Steingruber-Wildgans (Young Girl), Helmut Kretzschmar (Young Man), Horst Günter (a Man), Hermann Rieth (a Priest and Ephraimite), Ursula Zollenkopf (Invalid Woman), Dorothea Förster-Georgi, Karla Maria Pfeffer-Düring, Annemarie Tamm and Charlotte Betcke (Four Virgins), Dorothea Förster-Georgi, Maria Hüger, Ursula Zollenkopf, Hartwig Stuckmann, Horst Sellentin, Ernst-Max Lühr (six voices in the orchestra).

The first stage performance of the opera was given at the Stadttheater Zürich, on June 6, 1957, under the auspices of the Zürich June Festival. The production was in the hands of Karl Heinz Krahl, Paul Haferung and Jaroslav Berger; Hans Rosbaud was the musical director. Hans Erismann was in charge of the training of the following choral groups: the professional chorus of the Stadttheater Zürich, the chorus of the Stadttheater Lucerne (chorus-master Filip Raziag), members of the radio choir, Zürich, of the Zürcher Kammersprechchor (chorusmasters Ellen Widmann and Fred Barth). The orchestra was the Tonhalle-orchestra, Zürich. This was the cast: Hans Herbert Fiedler (Moses), Helmut Melchert (Aaron), Charles Gillig (Heathen Priest), Ingeborg Friedrich (Young Girl), Hans-Bert Dick (Young Man), Nikolaus Toth (Another Man), Charles Gillig (Israelite Priest), Adolf Diehn, Rudolf Gautschi, Paul Schriber (Three Elders), Ilse Wallenstein, Ingeborg Friedrich,

The 'Dance round the Golden Calf', in the Berlin Production, 1959

TWO SCENES FROM THE OPERA
IN THE BERLIN PRODUCTION, 1959

Irma Keller, Mary Davenport (Four Virgins); Mary Davenport (Invalid Woman), Rudolf Fiebelkorn (Youth), Willi Ferenz (Ephraimite), Ingeborg Friedrich, Irma Keller, Mary Davenport, Hans-Bert Dick, Nikolaus Toth, Charles Gillig (solo voices in the orchestra). There were four performances in all, on June 6, 8, 10 and 12.

To realize this unique work in performance, unique powers of artistry, energy and perseverance were needed. This, indeed, is why we think it fitting to put down here the names of the participants in these performances.

The third complete performance of the work, its second stage performance, took place at Berlin, Charlottenburg, at the Städtische Oper. The première on October 4, 1959, and the subsequent performances confirmed the impression made by the Zürich production: the audience succumbed to the spell of the unique. The Berlin performance was produced by Gustav Rudolf Sellner, and the scenery designed by Michel Raffaelli. As with every staging of the work, the Berlin production, too, had to face two fundamental issues. One concerns the realistic or, as the case may be, stylized representation of the composer's intentions, as they appear in the music. The second issue refers to the third act. In Zürich, it had been decided to close the performance with the end of the second act: the text of the third act was reproduced in the programme-book. In Berlin, the text of the third act was spoken on the stage by Moses and Aaron, in the manner of a spoken drama, while, as a very soft background, the music of the first scene was relayed through a loudspeaker. In Berlin, Hermann Scherchen was the conductor. Moses was spoken by Josef Greindl, and Aaron sung by Helmut Melchert.

Moses and Aaron is without precedent. It occupies a solitary prominence in our century, even allowing for the many other musical works that have been created as affirmations of religious faith.

What is its historical position?

The opera is a musical synthesis of all the forces in the history of Western music, from the Flemish composers, through Bach and the Viennese classics to Wagner and Brahms, gathered by, and filtered through, Schoenberg's creativity.

The work is at once dramatic and epic, opera and oratorio; its spontaneity never diminishes. The whole encompasses every level of belief, from closeness to God to heathen rites; it subsumes the world under a single idea—the divine idea. In the service of his idea, the composer uses a thousand-tongued orchestra, producing timbres and sound-combinations never heard before. These are never an end in themselves, but always subject to the idea of the whole. The opera is one of those works of which stage presentation can often no more than approach the idea that may have been in its creator's mind. But people will always be found with the courage to perform it.

As Bach's *St. Matthew Passion* gives artistic expression to the spirit of Christianity, so Schoenberg's *Moses and Aaron* gives artistic expression to the spirit of the Old Testament—both are avowals of faith. Like the *St. Matthew Passion*, too, *Moses and Aaron* is a religious confession in the medium of art. On an artistic level, both works also speak to those who do not stand on the ground of Old Testament or Christian theology. Moses' fate in Schoenberg's opera, his fight for truth, its recognition and dissemination, is a timeless aspect of human destiny.

Bibliography

Babbit, Milton, 'An Introduction to the Music', *Booklet for the LP records of the opera 'Moses and Aaron'*, Columbia, New York (these records are distributed by Philips in England).

Bach, David Josef, 'Du sollst nicht, du musst', *Arnold Schönberg zum 60. Geburtstag*, Universal Edition, Vienna, 1934.

Birke, Joachim, 'Richard Dehmel und Arnold Schönberg, ein Briefwechsel', *Die Musikforschung*, 11th year, vol. 3, 1958.

Gradenwitz, Peter, 'Schönbergs religiöse Werke', *Melos, Zeitschrift für Neue Musik*, 26th year, vol. 11, November 1959.

Gradenwitz, Peter, 'Gustav Mahler and Arnold Schoenberg', *Year Book V*, Leo Baeck Institute, London, 1960.

Jelinek, Hanns, *Anleitung zur Zwölftonkomposition*, Universal Edition, Vienna, 1952 (part 1) and 1958 (part II).

Kandinsky, Wassily, 'Die Bilder', *Arnold Schönberg* (contributions by Alban Berg, P. von Gütersloh, K. Horwitz, H. Jalowetz, W. Kandinsky, etc.), R. Piper and Co., Munich, 1912.

Keller, Hans, 'Schoenberg's "Moses and Aaron"', *The Score*, no. 21, October 1957.

Kerner, Dieter, 'Arnold Schönberg', *Medizinischer Monatsspiegel*, 8th year, vol. 5, May 1959.

Leibowitz, René, *Histoire de l'opéra*, ch. XXII ('Les oeuvres dramatiques d'Arnold Schoenberg'), Buchet-Chastel, Paris, 1957.

Leibowitz, René, *Introduction à la musique de douze sons*, L'Arche, Paris, 1949.

Leibowitz, René, *Schoenberg and His School*, trans. Dika Newlin, Philosophical Library, New York, 1949 (original French edition, *Schönberg et son école*, I. B. Janin, Paris, 1947).

Pfrogner, Hermann, *Die Zwölfordnung der Töne*, Amalthea-Verlag, Zürich, Leipzig and Vienna, 1953.

Rufer, Josef, *Composition with Twelve Notes*, trans. Humphrey Searle, Barrie and Rockliff, London, 1954.

Rufer, Josef, 'Rede auf Arnold Schönberg', *Melos, Zeitschrift für Neue Musik*, 24th year, vol. 12, December 1957.

Rufer, Josef, *The Works of Arnold Schoenberg*, trans. Dika Newlin, Faber and Faber, London, 1962.

Schering, Arnold, *Das Symbol in der Musik*, Koehler und Amelang, Leipzig, 1941.

Schoenberg, Arnold, *Letters*, selected and edited by Erwin Stein, B. Schott's Söhne, Mainz, 1958 (English edition in preparation, Faber and Faber, London).

Stuckenschmidt, H. H., *Arnold Schoenberg*, trans. Edith Temple Roberts and Humphrey Searle, John Calder, London, 1959.

Stuckenschmidt, H. H., 'Moderne Psalmen von Arnold Schönberg', *Österreichische Musikzeitschrift*, 12th year, vol. 2, February 1957.

Vlad, Roman, 'Moderne Psalmen von Schönberg', *Melos, Zeitschrift für Neue Musik*, 24th year, vol. 9, September 1957.

Wörner, Karl H., 'Arnold Schoenberg and the Theatre', *The Musical Quarterly*, vol. XLVIII, no. 4, October, 1962.

Wörner, Karl H., *Neue Musik in der Entscheidung*, B. Schott's Söhne, Mainz, 1956.

Wörner, Karl H., ' "Und trotzdem bete ich"; Arnold Schoenberg's letztes Werk, "Moderne Psalmen" ', *Neue Zeitschrift für Musik*, 118th year, vol. 3, March 1957.

Zillig, Winfried, 'Notes on Arnold Schoenberg's unfinished oratorio, "Die Jakobsleiter" ', *The Score*, no. 25, January 1959.

Zillig, Winfried, 'Schönberg's "Moses und Aron" ', *Melos, Zeitschrift für Neue Musik*, 24th year, vol. 3, March 1957.

Appendix: The Libretto

*(The English translation is by Allen Forte,
and is reproduced together with the original
German by kind permission of Mrs Gertrud
Schoenberg and B. Schott's Söhne, Mainz)*

ARNOLD SCHOENBERG, 'MOSES AND AARON'

Opera in Three Acts

DRAMATIS PERSONAE

Moses, *Speaking Role*
Aaron, *Tenor*
Young Girl, *Soprano*
Invalid Woman, *Alto*
Young Man, *Tenor*
Naked Youth, *Tenor*
Another Man, *Baritone*
Ephraimite, *Baritone*
Priest, *Bass*
Four Naked Virgins, 2 *Sopranos (one of them the Young Girl),*
    and 2 *Altos*
Voice from the Burning Bush, *Sopranos, Boys, Altos, Tenors,*
    Baritones, Basses, 3–6 to each part
Beggars, 6–8 *Altos,* 6–8 *Basses*
Several Elderly Persons, *Tenors*
Seventy Elders, *Basses, a third to be singers (about 25), the rest to*
    be supernumeraries

12 Tribal Chieftains, *1st and 2nd Tenors, 1st and 2nd Basses*
Chorus, *Large mixed chorus of Sopranos, Mezzo-Sopranos, Altos,
    Tenors, Baritones, Basses*
6 Solo Voices (in the orchestra), *Soprano, Mezzo-Soprano, Alto,
    Tenor, Baritone, Bass*
Dancers, Supernumeraries of all kinds

INSTRUMENTATION

3 Flutes	Timpani
all alt. Piccolo	Percussion:
3 Oboes	Snare Drum, Bass Drum,
3rd alt. English Horn	large Tenor Drum, Tam-
1 Clarinet in E flat	bourine, Cymbals, Tam-tam,
2 Clarinets in B flat and A	Gong, Triangle, Glocken-
1 Bass Clarinet in B flat and A	spiel, Xylophone, Flexatone,
2 Bassoons	high and low Bells, high
1 Contrabassoon	Bell without specific pitch,
4 Horns in F	Rattle
3 Trumpets in C	Harp
3 Trombones	Piano
1 Tuba	Celesta
Strings	2 Mandolins

INSTRUMENTS FOR THE STAGE MUSIC IN ACT II

1 Piccolo	Percussion:
1 Flute	Bass Drums (muffled),
1 English Horn	Tambourine, Gongs (high
1 Clarinet	and low), Cymbals,
1 Horn	Xylophone
2 Trumpets	Piano
3 Trombones	2 Mandolins
Timpani	2 Guitars

Libretto

I. AKT

1. SZENE: MOSES BERUFUNG

MOSES
> *Einziger, ewiger, allgegenwärtiger,*
> *unsichtbarer und unvorstellbarer Gott!*

DIE STIMME AUS DEM DORNBUSCH
> *Lege die Schuhe ab:*
> *bist weit genug gegangen;*
> *du stehst auf heiligem Boden;*
> *nun verkünde!*

MOSES
> *Gott meiner Väter, Gott Abrahams,*
> *Isaaks und Jakobs, der du ihren Gedanken*
> *in mir wiedererweckt hast, mein Gott,*
> *nötige mich nicht, ihn zu verkünden.*
> *Ich bin alt; laß mich in Ruhe meine*
> *Schafe weiden!*

DIE STIMME
> *Du hast die Greuel gesehn, die Wahrheit*
> *erkannt: so kannst du nicht anders mehr:*
> *du mußt dein Volk daraus befrein!*

MOSES
> *Wer bin ich, mich der Macht der Blindheit*
> *entgegenzustellen?*

DIE STIMME
> *Dem einzigen Gott verbunden,*

ACT I

SCENE 1: THE CALLING OF MOSES

MOSES
Only one, infinite, thou omnipresent one,
unperceived and inconceivable God!

VOICE FROM THE BURNING BUSH
Here lay your shoes aside.
You have gone far enough now.
You stand on ground that is holy.
Be God's prophet!

MOSES
God of my fathers, of Abraham, Isaac, and
Jacob, who has once more awakened their
great thoughts in my own mind, O God,
ask not thy servant to be thy prophet. I am
old. I ask thee, let me tend my sheep in
silence.

VOICE
You've seen your kindred enslaved, the
truth you have known, so you can do nothing else:
therefore you must set your folk free!

MOSES
Who am I to combat the power and force
of that blindness?

VOICE
United with God in oneness,

H

mit dir einig,
mit Pharao entzweit!

MOSES

Was bezeugt dem Volk meinen Auftrag?

DIE STIMME

Des Einzigen Name!
Der Ewige will es befrein, daß es nicht
mehr Vergänglichem diene.

MOSES

Niemand wird mir glauben

DIE STIMME

Vor ihren Ohren wirst du Wunder tun—
ihre Augen werden sie anerkennen:
von deinem Stab werden sie hören—
deine Klugheit bewundern;
von deiner Hand—
an deine Kraft glauben,
vom Wasser des Nil—
fühlen, was ihrem Blut befohlen.

MOSES

Meine Zunge ist ungelenk:
ich kann denken,
aber nicht reden.

DIE STIMME

Wie aus diesem Dornbusch,
finster, eh das Licht
der Wahrheit auf ihn fiel,
so vernimmst du meine Stimme
aus jedem Ding.
Aron will ich erleuchten,

to him joined,
from Pharaoh torn loose!

MOSES

What will give them proof of my mandate?

VOICE

The name of one holy!
The infinite will set them free;
they shall no longer perish in bondage.

MOSES

No one will believe me!

VOICE

Before their ears you shall do wondrous things.
And their eyes will see you and recognize you.
And by your rod will they behold you,
and admire your great wisdom!
Then by your hand
they will believe your power
and feel in the Nile waters
what their own blood commands them.

MOSES

But my tongue is not flexible:
thought is easy;
speech is laborious.

VOICE

E'en as from this bush,
in darkness, ere the light
of truth fell thereupon,
so will you perceive my message
in everything.
    Aaron will be enlightened,

er soll dein Mund sein!
Aus ihm soll deine Stimme sprechen,
wie aus dir die meine!
Und ihr werdet gesegnet sein.
Denn das gelobe ich dir:
Dieses Volk ist auserwählt,
vor allen Völkern,
das Volk des einzigen Gottes zu sein,
daß es ihn erkenne
und sich ihm allein ganz widme;
daß es alle Prüfungen bestehe,
denen in Jahrtausenden
der Gedanke ausgesetzt ist.
Und das verheiße ich dir:
Ich will euch dorthin führen,
wo ihr mit dem Ewigen einig
und allen Völkern ein Vorbild werdet.
Und nun gehe!
Aron triffst du in der Wüste.
Er kommt dir auf deinem Weg entgegen;
daran sollst du ihn erkennen.
Verkünde!

2. SZENE: MOSES BEGEGNET ARON IN DER WÜSTE

ARON

> *Du Sohn meiner Väter,*
> *schickt dich mir der große Gott?*

MOSES

> *Du Sohn meines Vaters, Bruder des Geistes,*
> *aus dem der Einzige sprechen will:*

Note: Brackets indicate passages where two

he shall be your mouth!
From him will your own voice then issue,
as from you comes my voice!
And your people will now be blest,
for this I promise to you:
Your folk are the chosen ones
before all others.
They are the folk of the one God alone.
They are thus to know him
and give him alone their worship.
Also they will undergo all hardships
that have in millennia
ever come to be conceived.
And this I promise to you:
I shall conduct you forward
to where with the infinite oneness
you'll be a model to every nation.
Now begone hence.
Aaron nears you in the wasteland.
You soon will see him approach and greet him.
Of this you are to inform him.
Go forth now!

SCENE 2: MOSES MEETS AARON IN THE WASTELAND

AARON
O son of my fathers,
are you sent by mighty God?

MOSES
O son of my father, brother in spirit,
through whom the only one is to speak,

or more characters are heard simultaneously.

117

Vernimm mich und ihn; und sage,
was du verstehst!

ARON

Mein Bruder, gab der Allmächtige mich dir
als Gefäß, auszuschütten über unsre Brüder
des Ewigen Gnade?

MOSES

Gnade schenkt er dir aus Erkenntnis.

ARON

Glückliches Volk, einem einzigen Gott
zu gehören, den zu bekämpfen kein andrer
Macht besitzt.

MOSES

Andre gibt es nur im Menschen, nur in
der Vorstellung.
In ihr hat der Allgegenwärtige nicht Raum.

ARON

Gebilde der höchsten Phantasie, wie dankt
sie dir's, daß du sie reizest zu bilden!

MOSES

Kein Bild kann dir ein Bild geben vom
Unvorstellbaren.

ARON

Nie wird Liebe ermüden, sich's vorzubilden.
Glückliches Volk, das so seinen Gott liebt.

MOSES

Volk, auserwählt, den Unsichtbaren zu wissen,
den Unvorstellbaren zu denken.

now hear me, and him, and tell me
    what you perceive.

AARON

My brother, did the almighty one give
you me as his vessel, that from it be
poured forth on our brothers
the infinite's holy grace?

MOSES

Grace is granted through recognition.

AARON

O happy folk, to have one mighty god
to belong to, against whose forces no other
power prevails.

MOSES

Others live within a people, only
    in fantasy;
but God the Almighty exists apart from men.

AARON

O vision of highest fantasy, how glad
it is that you've enticed it to form you.

MOSES

How can fantasy thus picture the
    unimageable?

AARON

Love will surely not weary of image forming.
Happy is this folk to revere its God so!

MOSES

Folk set apart to know the ever-unseen one,
to reflect on greatness unimaged.

ARON

Auserwähltes Volk,
einen einzigen Gott ewig zu lieben
mit tausendmal mehr der Liebe,
mit der alle andern Völker ihre vielen Götter
lieben.
Unsichtbar! Unvorstellbar!
Volk, auserwählt dem Einzigen, kannst du
lieben, was du dir nicht vorstellen darfst?

MOSES

Darfst? Unvorstellvar, weil unsichtbar;
weil unüberblickbar;
weil unendlich;
weil ewig;
weil allgegenwärtig;
weil allmächtig.
Nur einer ist allmächtig.

ARON

Unvorstellbarer Gott:
Du strafst die Sünden der Väter an den
Kindern und Kindeskindern!

MOSES

Strafst du?
Sind wir fähig, zu verursachen, was dich
zu Folgen nötigt?

ARON

Gerechter Gott:
Du belohnst die, die deinen Geboten
gehorchen!

MOSES

Gerechter Gott:

120

AARON

Chosen is this folk,
thus to love one great god ever and ever,
with a thousand times more devotion
than all other earthly peoples for their many
 godly beings.
Not be seen, not imagined.
Folk chosen by the only one, can you
worship what you dare not even conceive?

MOSES

Dare not? Not conceived because unseen,
can never be measured,
everlasting,
eternal,
because ever present,
and almighty.
The one God is almighty.

AARON

Inconceivable God:
Thou punisheth sins of the father on his
children and children's children.

MOSES

Punish?
Are we able to originate what thou
demand'st as outcome?

AARON

O righteous God:
Thou rewardest those who are faithful
 to thy commandments!

MOSES

O righteous God:

121

Du hast gerichtet,
wie alles geschehen soll:
Gebührt dem Lohn, der gern anders möchte?
Oder dem, der nichts andres vermag?

ARON

Gütiger Gott!
Du erhörst die Bitten der Armen,
nimmst an die Opfer der Guten!

MOSES

Allmächtiger Gott,
dich erkauften die Opfer der Armen,
die du arm gemacht hast?
Reinige dein Denken,
lös es von Wertlosem,
weihe es Wahrem:
kein andrer Gewinn dankt deinem Opfer.

ARON

Nur ein allmächtiger Gott konnte
solch ein schwaches, gedemütigtes Volk
auserwählen, seine Allmacht, seine Wunder
an ihm zu zeigen,
es zu lehren,
an ihn allein zu glauben.

MOSES

Unerbittliches Denkgesetz
zwingt zur Erfüllung.

ARON

Allmächtiger!
Sei der Gott dieses Volkes!
Befrei es aus Pharaos
Knechtschaft!

Thou has directed
how everything must befall.
Then to whom is the reward presented,
him who wants or cannot want things else?

AARON

How good thou art!
Thou perceiv'st the pleas of the beggars,
tak'st up the off'rings made by the good.

MOSES

O almighty God,
do the off'rings of beggars then buy thee,
who thyself made them poor?
Purify your thinking.
Free it from worthless things.
Let it be righteous.
No other reward is giv'n your off'rings.

AARON

Only this almighty God could
select a people so weak and so downtrodden,
and to them exhibit all his might and his
great wonders,
and teach them how they should learn
to revere him and him alone give credence.

MOSES

Law of thought irresistible
forces fulfilment.

AARON

Almighty one,
be the god of this people;
release them from Pharaoh's
harsh bondage.

3. SZENE: MOSES UND ARON VERKÜNDEN DEM VOLK DIE BOTSCHAFT GOTTES

JUNGES MÄDCHEN
Ich hab ihn gesehn,
als eine feurige Flamme aufschlug,
die ihn rief!
Er warf sich auf die Knie
und verbarg sein Antlitz im Sand.
Dann zog er in die Wüste.

JUNGER MANN
Bei meinem Haus,
wie eine leuchtende Wolke,
kam er eben vorbei.
Er schwebte mehr, als er ging,
kaum berührt' sein Fuß den Weg,
und rasch schwand er dem Auge.

ANDRER MANN
Ich frug ihn,
aber er beachtet' mich nicht;
lief weiter, und dennoch hörte ich:
ein Gott habe ihm befohlen,
seinen Bruder Moses
in der Wüste zu treffen.

PRIESTER
Moses?
Der den Fronvogt erschlug?

CHOR (Frauen und Männer)
Moses!
Er flüchtete!

SCENE 3: MOSES AND AARON BRING GOD'S MESSAGE TO THE PEOPLE

A YOUNG GIRL
> I saw him afar,
> just as a flame hotly glowing sprang forth
> and addressed him.
> He threw himself on his knees
> and concealed his face in the sand.
> He then went forth in the wasteland.

A YOUNG MAN
> He passed by my house
> as would a luminous cloud pass,
> even so came he by.
> He floated rather than walked.
> Hardly indeed did he touch the ground.
> He quickly passed from my vision.

ANOTHER MAN
> I hailed him,
> but he neither gave me a sign
> nor tarried. And then I heard it said
> a god had commanded that he
> meet his brother, Moses,
> in the region of the wasteland.

PRIEST
> Moses?
> He who murdered the guard?

CHORUS (*Men and Women*)
> Moses!
> He ran away!

Uns ereilte die Rache Pharaos!
Kommt er wieder, Aufruhr zu stiften?

PRIESTER
Mit einem neuen Gott verbündet!

CHOR (Frauen)
Ein neuer Gott: Neue Opfer!

MANN
Er wird uns beschützen!

PRIESTER
Die alten Götter haben auch beschützt.
Tat's der eine nicht,
wandte man sich an den andern.

CHOR (Frauen)
Man kann von den Göttern auch
nichts Unmögliches verlangen.

JUNGER MANN
Wie er wohl aussehn mag, der neue Gott?
Er schwebt wohl, da auch Aron schwebte.

MANN
Der neue Gott,
vielleicht ist er stärker als Pharao?
Stärker als unsere Götter?
Die anderen Götter helfen
nur den Bedrückern.
Das ist der Gott, der uns hilft.

MÄDCHEN
Ich glaube,
es muß ein lieblicher Gott sein,

We then suffered the wrath of Pharaoh!
Now returning, will he stir rebellion?

PRIEST

Are we now bound to serve a new god?

CHORUS (*Women*)

Another god: other off'rings!

MAN

He'll be our protector!

PRIEST

The olden gods did also give protection.
And if one did fail,
prayers were made unto the others.

CHORUS (*Women*)

O ask not the gods, then,
impossibility's fulfilment.

A YOUNG MAN

How will he look to us, the newest god?
It's certain that he soars, for Aaron did.

MAN

The newest god
perhaps will be stronger than Pharaoh,
stronger than our other gods are.
The gods in the past have aided
those who oppressed us.
This god will come to our aid.

GIRL

I know that
he shall be pleasing and youthful,

iung und schön und glänzend,
da doch Aron so glänzte.

CHOR

    Soll man ihn nach diesem Moses beurteilen,
    so wird er Blutopfer fordern.
    Der neue Gott wird uns auch nicht helfen!
    Blutopfer! Blutopfer!

PRIESTER

    Lästre nicht!
    Es gibt Götter, die nur strafen
    und solche, die nur belohnen.
    Manche muß man öfter versöhnen,
    andre kann man sich dauernd gewinnen.

CHOR (in vielen kleinen Gruppen)
    Blutopfer! Blutopfer!

MÄDCHEN

    Wie macht er mich froh!
    Wie schwellt das Glück mein Herz!
    Jubel füllt meine Seele!
    Anbetungswürdiger Gott,
    zeige dich mir in deiner Schönheit:
    Ich will in Liebe dir dienen.

JUNGER MANN

    Du schwebender Gott,
    hoch in den Höhen des Himmels,
    höher als andre Götter:
    Erhebst du uns zu dir,
    neben dich: wie schwindet die Macht
    der falschen, ohnmächtigen Abgötter.

MANN

    Hilft er uns,

handsome in his splendour,
and will gleam as did Aaron.

CHORUS
If we are by this man, Moses, to judge the god,
then are some blood off'rings needed.
The newest god also will not help us!
Blood off'rings! Blood off'rings!

PRIEST
Blaspheme not!
There are gods who only punish,
and those gods who only favour.
Many often must be appeased;
others can be won over forever.

CHORUS (*in many small groups*)
Blood off'rings! Blood off'rings!

GIRL
He makes me so glad!
My heart is swelled with joy!
Joyousness fills my spirit!
O holy, worshipful God,
be thou revealed in all thy glory.
I serve in love of thy greatness.

A YOUNG MAN
O god that soars high,
high in the heights of the heavens,
higher than other gods do:
O lift us up to thee,
nigh to thee. How quickly depart
the power and might of false images!

MAN
If he aids,

schützt er uns gegen die Knechte Pharaos
und gegen seine falschen Götter:
soll er unser Gott sein,
Gott der Kinder Israels,
dem wir dienen, dem wir opfern.

CHOR (in vielen Gruppen)
Ein lieblicher Gott!
Er zeigt sich in Schönheit!
Ein schwebender Gott!
Er hebt uns zu sich!
Ein rettender Gott!
Er wird uns befrein!
Vielleicht ist er stärker als Pharao!
Glaubt den Betrügern nicht!
Wir wollen ihm dienen!
Wir wollen ihm opfern!
Wir wollen ihn lieben!

CHOR (in zwei Gruppen)
Glaubt nicht den Bertrügern!
Die Götter lieben uns nicht!
Wer ist es, der stärker sein
will, als Pharaos Götter?
Laßt uns in Frieden!
Zurück zur Arbeit!
Sonst wird sie noch schwerer!
Er wird uns befrein!
Wir wollen ihn lieben!
Wir wollen ihm opfern!
Wir wollen ihn lieben!
Wir wollen ihm opfern!

MÄDCHEN
Er wird uns befrein!

if he shields us from the men of Pharaoh
and also shields us from his false gods,
then he shall be our God
and the God of Israel,
whom we serve, to whom we make off'rings.

CHORUS (*in many groups*)
A god that will please,
revealed in his glory!
A god that can soar,
that takes us to him!
A god that will save!
He shall make us free!
Perhaps he is stronger than Pharaoh!
Heed not the lying ones!
We give him obedience!
We want to make off'rings,
We want to worship him.

CHORUS (*in two groups*)
O heed not the liars!
The gods do not give us love!
Who is this would mightier be
than Pharaoh's gods are?
Leave us in peace now!
Continue working,
lest it become harder!
He shall make us free!
We want to give worship!
We want to make off'rings!
We want to give worship!
We want to make off'rings!

GIRL
He shall make us free!

(Moses und Aron, in weiter Ferne
auftauchend, kommen allmählich näher,
auf solche Weise, wie die Chöre es
beschreiben.)

CHOR

Seht Moses und Aron!
Moses' mächtiges Haupt!
Moses, den Stab in der Hand,
schreitet langsam, bedächtig,
scheint fast zu stehn,
bewegt sich kaum.

Steht Moses, oder geht er?
Moses steht!
Nein, er schreitet langsam!
Er steht!
Nein, er geht!
Mächtig sein weißes Haupt,
gewaltig sein Arm!
Gewaltig sein Haupt!
Seht!
Aron, gewiß nicht mehr jung,
eilt beschwingt, leichten Schrittes
weit vor ihm her
und steht doch nah bei ihm!
Steht Aron jetzt bei Moses?
Nein, er eilt voran!
Geht Aron an Moses Seite?
Vor oder hinter ihm?
Sie bewegen sich nicht im Raum.
Sind näher,
sind ferner,
sind tiefer,
sind höher—
verschwinden gänzlich!

(Far in the distance Moses and Aaron
suddenly appear. They approach in the
manner described by the choruses.)

CHORUS

See Moses and Aaron!
Moses' powerful head!
Moses, his rod in his hand,
moving slowly, reflective,
seems to stand still,
now moves somewhat.

Does he wait? Is he moving?
Moses waits!
No, he's walking slowly!
He waits!
No, he moves!
Mighty his whitened head,
and strong is his arm!
And strong is his mien!
See!
Aaron, a young man no more,
moves along with a light step
far before him,
and yet stands close to him!
Is Aaron close to Moses?
No, he goes before!
Is Aaron at Moses' side now?
Front or in back of him?
They are moving, but not in space.
Are nearer,
are farther,
are deeper,
are higher—
have vanished wholly!

Seht Moses! Seht Aron!
Sie sind jetzt da!

4. SZENE

CHOR (alle)
> *Bringt ihr Erhörung,*
> *Botschaft des neuen Gottes?*
> *Schickt er als Führer*
> *euch uns zu neuer Hoffnung?*
> *Gern wollen wir ihm*
> *Geld, Gut und Leben opfern!*
> *Nehmt, fragt nicht lange:*
> *Selbstliebe zwingt uns, drängt uns,*
> *uns ihm zu geben,*
> *Aussicht nicht nur auf Gnade;*
> *Hingabe selbst ist*
> *Wollust, ist höchste Gnade!*

MOSES
> *Der Einzige, Ewige, Allmächtige,*
> *Allgegenwärtige, Unsichtbare,*
> *Unvorstellbare . . .*

ARON
> *Er hat euch vor allen Völkern*
> *auserwählt . . .*

MOSES
> *. . . verlangt kein Opfer von euch:*

ARON
> *. . . und will euch allein . . .*

134

See Moses! See Aaron!
They have arrived!

SCENE 4

CHORUS (*all*)
>Bring you good tidings,
>word from the mighty new god?
>Come you to lead us,
>Once more to make us hopeful?
>We yearn to give him
>gold, goods, and living off'rings!
>Take, do not ask us.
>Self-love compels us, forces us
>to make off'rings,
>not only for his favour;
>giving itself is
>pleasure, the highest favour!

MOSES
>The only one, infinite, all-powerful one,
>the omnipresent one, invisible,
>inconceivable . . .

AARON
>He's chosen this folk before all
>other people . . .

MOSES
>. . . demands no off'ring from you.

AARON
>. . . and gives you alone . . .

MOSES

> . . . er will nicht den Teil,
> er fordert das Ganze.

ARON

> . . . seine ganze Gnade schenken.
> Werft euch nieder, ihn anzubeten!

CHOR

> Anbeten? Wen? Wo ist er?
> Ich sehe ihn nicht!
> Wo ist er?
> Sieht er gut oder böse aus?
> Sollen wir ihn lieben oder fürchten?
> Wo ist er?
> Zeig ihn uns! So wollen wir knien!
> So wollen wir Vieh herschleppen
> und Gold und Getreide und Wein!
> Alles soll euer Gott bekommen,
> wenn wir sein Volk sind,
> wenn er unser Gott ist,
> wenn er uns beschützt!
> Aber wo ist er?
> Zeig ihn uns!

ARON

> Schließet die Augen,
> verstopfet die Ohren!
> So nur könnt ihr ihn sehn und hören!
> Kein Lebender sieht und hört ihn anders

CHOR

> Ist er niemals zu sehn?
> Ist er ewig unsichtbar?

CHOR (Frauen)

> Wie? Dein allmächtiger Gott
> kann sich uns nicht sichtbar machen?

MOSES

... He wants not a part,
for everything's wanted.

AARON

... his unbounded holy favour.
On your knees, then, to give him worship!

CHORUS

To worship, whom? Where is he?
But I see him not!
Where is he?
Has he gentle or angry mien?
Are we then to love him or to fear him?
Where is he?
Point him out! We want to kneel down.
We want to bring beasts forth to him,
and gold, wheat and barley, and wine!
All will go to your God almighty,
if we're his people,
if he is our god now and
if he guards us well!
But then where is he?
Point him out!

AARON

Close off your vision
and stop up your hearing!
For in this way shall you see and hear him!
No living man otherwise perceives him!

CHORUS

Can he never be seen?
Is he never visible?

CHORUS (*Women*)

He, your most mighty of gods,
cannot show himself before us?

137

ARON
> *Der Gerechte sieht ihn.*

MÄDCHEN
> *Ich sah seinen Glanz!*

JUNGER MANN
> *Du schwebender Gott!*

MANN
> *Er ist unser Gott!*

PRIESTER
> *Dann braucht ihn der Mörder nicht*
> *zu fürchten!*

ARON
> *Wer ihn nicht sieht, ist verloren!*

CHOR (Männer)
> *So sind wir alle verloren,*
> *denn wir sehen ihn nicht!*

> (Lachen.)

CHOR
> *Bleib uns fern mit deinem Gott,*
> *mit dem Allmächtigen!*
> *Wir wollen durch ihn nicht befreit sein!*
> *Bleib uns so fern wie dein Gott,*
> *der Allgegenwärtige!*
> *Wir fürchten und lieben ihn nicht!*
> *So wenig als er uns belohnt und bestraft!*

MOSES
> *Allmächtiger, meine Kraft ist zu Ende:*

AARON

But the righteous shall see him.

GIRL

I saw how he gleamed!

YOUNG MAN

He soars as a god!

MAN

He must be our god!

PRIEST

Then why need the murd'rer ever
fear him?

AARON

Who sees him not is forsaken!

CHORUS (*Men*)

Then we must all be forsaken,
since we still see him not!

(*Laughter.*)

CHORUS

Keep away with your new god,
with this almighty one!
Through him we do not want our freedom!
Keep far away, like your god,
the all-present deity!
We fear not, nor love we your god;
so little does he give reward or chastise!

MOSES

Almighty one, now my strength is exhausted,

Mein Gedanke ist machtlos
in Arons Wort!

(Moses immer weiter im Hintergrund.)

6 SOLOSTIMMEN
  Aron!

ARON
  Schweige!
  Das Wort bin ich und die Tat!

(Er entreißt Moses den Stab.)

CHOR
  Aron, was tust du?

ARON
  Dieser Stab führt euch:
  Seht, die Schlange!

(Wirft den Stab zu Boden.)

CHOR
  Flieht! Die Schlange wächst!
  Sie dreht sich!
  Seht! Sie wendet sich gegen alle!

ARON
  In Moses' Hand ein starrer Stab: das Gesetz;
  in meiner Hand die bewegliche Schlange:
     die Klugheit.
  Stellt euch so, wie sie euch zwingt!

CHOR
  Weicht, zieht euch zurück!
  Kommt hierher, geht dorthin!

and my thought become powerless
in Aaron's word!

(*Moses more and more in the background.*)

6 SOLO VOICES
Aaron!

AARON
Silence!
The word is mine and the deed!

(*He tears the rod from Moses' hand.*)

CHORUS
Aaron, what's happening?

AARON
Moses' rod leads you.
Look, a serpent!

(*Throws the rod to the ground.*)

CHORUS
Flee! The serpent grows!
It's twisting!
See, it's turning now 'gainst the people!

AARON
In Moses' hand a rigid rod: this, the law.
In my own hand the most supple of serpents:
  discretion.
Now stand so, as it commands!

CHORUS
Move! Go farther back!
Come this way! Go that way!

Verteilt euch besser!
Vergebens, sie hält uns in Bann!

(Aron nimmt die Schlange beim Schwanz, legt
sie als Stab wieder in Moses Hand.)

ARON
Erkennet die Macht,
die dieser Stab
dem Führer verleiht!

CHOR (Frauen, sprechend)
Ein Wunder erfüllt uns mit Schrecken:
Der Stab, der sich wandelt zur Schlange,
zeigt Aron als Herrn dieses Volkes.
Wie groß ist die Macht dieses Aron!

CHOR (Männer, singend)
Ist Aron der Knecht dieses Moses,
und Moses der Knecht seines Gottes,
so muß es ein mächtiger Gott sein,
da mächtige Knechte ihm dienen!

CHOR (alle)
Ist Aron der Knecht dieses Moses,
und Moses der Knecht seines Gottes,
durch den Stab, den sein Gott ihm gegeben,
ist mächtiger Moses als Aron,
so muß es ein mächtiger Gott sein,
der Starke zu zwingen vermag!
Wie groß ist die Macht dieses Gottes,
da mächtige Knechte ihm dienen!
Ist Aron der Knecht dieses Moses,
und Moses der Knecht seines Gottes,
so muß es ein mächtiger Gott sein,
da mächtige Knechte ihm dienen!

Take other places!
We're helpless. It has us in bonds!

(*Aaron takes the snake by the tail and puts it
back, as a rod, into Moses' hand.*)

AARON
You thus know the might
that through this rod
is imparted to the leader.

CHORUS (*Women, speaking*)
A marvel has filled us with terror.
The rod that did change to a serpent,
shows Aaron as lord of this people.
How great is the might of this Aaron!

CHORUS (*Men, singing*)
Is Aaron the servant of Moses?
Does Moses in turn serve this new god?
Then surely this god must be mighty,
when such mighty persons do serve him!

CHORUS (*all*)
Is Aaron the servant of Moses?
Does Moses in turn serve this new god?
Through the rod that his god gave to Moses
he's mightier even than Aaron.
Then surely this god must be mighty,
who even such strength can command.
How vast is the might of this great god,
when such mighty persons do serve him!
Is Aaron the servant of Moses?
Does Moses in turn serve this new god?
Then surely this god must be mighty,
when such mighty persons do serve him!

MÄDCHEN

Er wird uns befrein!

JUNGER MANN

Wir wollen ihm dienen!

MANN

Wir wollen ihm opfern!

PRIESTER

Dein Stab zwingt uns,
doch Pharao zwingt er nicht,
uns freizulassen!

ARON

Euer Mut ist gebrochen;
euer Stolz geschwunden;
ohne Hoffnung dient ihr
und glaubt nicht an euch,
noch an Gott.
Euer Herz ist krank!
So zwingt ihr Pharao nicht!

CHOR

Stark is Pharao!
Schwach sind wir!

ARON

Seht Moses' Hand:
gesund ist sie und stark.
Aber Moses' Herz gleicht eurem jetzt,
weil er euch schwach weiß und mutlos.
Führt er die Hand an dies Herz,
das krank ist, wie eures,
seht!

GIRL

> He shall make us free!

YOUNG MAN

> We want to give worship!

MAN

> We want to make off'rings!

PRIEST

> Your rod compels us,
> yet it does not compel Pharaoh
> to give us freedom!

AARON

> Oh, your spirit has been broken
> and your pride is shrunken.
> Hoping not, you labour,
> have no faith in God
> or yourselves,
> for your heart is sick!
> This way you'll not vanquish Pharaoh!

CHORUS

> Pharaoh is powerful:
> we are weak!

AARON

> See Moses' hand.
> So hale it is, and strong.
> But now Moses' heart is like your own,
> because he knows you lack spirit.
> Placing his hand on the heart,
> that's sick just as yours is,
> see!

K   145

CHOR

Aussatz! Flieht!
Weicht ihm aus!
Berührt ihn nicht!
Ihr werdet krank!
Aussatz!

ARON

Erkennt euch darin:
Mutlos, krank, verachtet,
geknechtet, gepeinigt!
Jetzt aber wohnt in Moses' Busen
der Geist des starken Gottes,
der Pharao zwingt,
den Frondienst aufzuheben.
Seht!

6 SOLOSTIMMEN

Seht!

ARON

Führt Moses nun an dies starke Herz
die aussätzige kranke Hand . . .

CHOR

Wunder! Seht! Wunder!
Gesund ist die Hand und stark!

ARON

Erkennet euch auch darin:
Euer Mut wird Pharao besiegen!

CHOR (Frauen)

Durch Aron läßt Moses uns sehen,
Wie er seinen Gott selbst erschaut hat,
so wird dieser Gott uns vorstellbar,
den sichtbare Wunder bezeugen.

CHORUS

>Leprous! Flee!
>Shun his path!
>And touch him not;
>you will be sick!
>Leprous!

AARON

>Therein see yourselves:
>downcast, sick, detested,
>enslaved, tormented!
>Now, even there in Moses' bosom
>the spirit of the great God dwells,
>that soon will force
>this Pharaoh to release you.
>See!

6 SOLO VOICES

>See!

AARON

>Moses now places that leprous hand
>upon his strong and healthy heart . . .

CHORUS

>Marvel! See! Marvel!
>The hand is now hale and strong!

AARON

>Discover therein your likeness.
>For your spirit shall defeat the hosts of Pharaoh.

CHORUS (*Women*)

>Through Aaron this Moses has shown us
>how he saw his god be revealed.
>And now can this god be imagined,
>attested by visible wonders.

147

CHOR (Männer)

Ein Wunder führt Aron vor Augen:
Die Hand die gesund oder krank wird,
ist Zeichen vom Wesen des Gottes,
der nicht sich uns selbst will zeigen!
Durch Aron läßt Moses uns sehen,
wie er seinen Gott selbst erschaut hat:
aussätzig die Hand des Ungläub'gen,
gesund dessen Herz, der dem Gott traut:
so wird dieser Gott uns vorstellbar.
Das Sinnbild erweitert zum Abbild sich,
das Herz glaubt voll Mut einem Gotte,
den sichtbare Wunder bezeugen.
Durch Aron läßt Moses uns sehen,
wie er seinen Gott selbst erschaut hat,
so wird dieser Gott uns vorstellbar,
den sichtbare Wunder bezeugen.

CHOR

Allmächt'ger Gott!

MANN UND CHOR (Männer)

Alles für die Freiheit!
Laßt uns die Ketten zerbrechen!
Erschlagt die Fronvögte!
Erschlagt sie!
Erschlagt ihre Priester!
Erschlagt sie!
Zerschlagt ihre Götter!
Zerschlagt sie!
Auf in die Wüste!

CHOR (Frauen)

Auf in die Wüste!

PRIESTER

Wahnsinnige!
Wovon soll euch die Wüste nähren?

Chorus (*Men*)

O Aaron has shown us a marvel.
The hand that can be hale or sickly
is proof of the being of this god,
who yet will not show his visage!
Through Aaron this Moses has shown us
how he saw his god be revealed.
O leprous the hands of the faithless,
and healthy the hearts of believers,
and now can this god be imagined.
The symbol enlarges to image him.
The spirited heart trusts in one god,
attested by visible wonders.
Through Aaron this Moses has shown us
how he saw his god be revealed.
And now can this god be imagined,
attested by visible wonders.

Chorus

Almighty God!

Man and Chorus (*Men*)

Everything for freedom!
Now let us shatter the shackles!
And kill the taskmasters!
Let's kill them!
And kill all their priesthood!
Let's kill them!
Destroy all their idols!
Destroy them!
Off to the wasteland!

Chorus (*Women*)

Off to the wasteland!

Priest

Madmen you are!
How can the wasteland give you nurture?

MOSES

> In der Wüste wird euch die Reinheit
> des Denkens nähren, erhalten
> und entwickeln . . .

ARON

> . . . und der Ewige läßt euch sehn
> ein Abbild eures leiblichen Glücks
> in jedem geistigen Wunder.
> Der Allwissende weiß, daß ihr ein Volk
> von Kindern seid
> und erwartet von Kindern nicht,
> was Großen schwierig.
> Er rechnet damit, daß alle Kinder reifen
> und alle Greise weise werden.
> Er gibt euch Frist, euer Leben in Freude
> der Vorbereitung auf die Weisheit des
> Alters zu widmen.
> Er wird es euch auch in der Wüste an Speise
> nicht fehlen lassen.
> Der Allmächtige verwandelt
> Sand in Frucht,
> Frucht in Gold,
> Gold in Wonne,
> Wonne in Geist.
> Wer speist den Nil,
> der dies Land ernährt?
> Er, der den Stab in die Schlange,
> Gesundheit in Aussatz verwandelt.
> Seht des Niles Wasser
> in diesem Krug! (Gießt es aus.)
> Nein: Ihr irrt euch nicht:
> Was ihr jetzt seht, ist Blut!
> Versteht ihr das?
> Es ist euer Blut, das dies Land ernährt,

MOSES

In the wasteland pureness of thought
will provide you nurture, sustain you
and advance you . . .

AARON

. . . and the only one lets you see
an image of your earthly good fortune
in every spiritual marvel.
The all-knowing one knows that you are still
a childlike folk
and does not expect from a child
what's hard for elders.
He reasons this way: that every child grows older,
and every elder shall be wiser.
He grants you time to devote to the pleasure
of preparation and the wisdom that
agedness will bring with it.
He never will fail to provide you with food
in the distant wasteland.
The almighty one can change
mere sand to fruit,
fruit to gold,
gold to rapture,
rapture to soul.
Who feeds the Nile,
that nurtures this land?
He, who did change rod to serpent
and changed health to leprosy's terror.
See the Nile's clear water
within this jar. (*Pours it out.*)
No, you are not wrong.
What you now see is blood!
What does this mean?
This is your own blood, that gives the
land nurture,

wie das Wasser des Nil.
Fett macht ihr die Knechte der Lüge,
der falschen Götter.   CHOR
Doch der Allmächtige befreit   *Auserwählt,*
euch und euer Blut.   *auserwählt!*
Er hat euch auserwählt vor allen Völkern,
das Volk des einzigen Gotts zu sein;
ihm allein zu dienen,
keines andern Knecht!
Ihr werdet frei sein
von Fron und Plage!
Das gelobt er euch:
Er wird euch führen in das Land,
wo Milch und Honig fließt;
und ihr sollt genießen leiblich,
was euren Vätern verheißen geistig.
Doch was Pharao bleibt,
seht her, ist wieder das
klare Wasser des Nil.
Und darin wird er untergehn!

CHOR

Er hat uns auserwählt vor allen Völkern,
das Volk des einz'gen Gotts zu sein;
ihm allein zu dienen,
keines andern Knecht!
Wir werden frei sein
von Fron und Plage!
Das gelobt er uns:
Er wird uns führen in das Land,
wo Milch und Honig fließt,
und wir soll'n genießen,
was er unsern Vätern verheißen.
Allmächt'ger, du bist stärker
als Ägyptens Götter,

as the flow of the Nile.
You fatten the servants of falsehood,
the slaves of false gods.   CHORUS
But the almighty one will free   Chosen folk,
you and free your blood.   chosen folk!
For he has chosen you over other peoples
to be the people of God alone,
him alone to worship,
in no other's service!
You will be free then
from toil and misery!
This is his promise:
He will then lead you to a land
where milk and honey flow.
There you shall have earthly pleasure
from what in spirit was vowed your fathers.
What for Pharaoh remains,
look here, is once more
the Nile's clear water alone.
And therein is he sure to drown.

CHORUS

We are his chosen folk before all others,
We are the chosen ones,
him alone to worship,
him alone to serve.
We shall be free then
from toil and misery!
This is his promise:
He will then lead us to a land
where milk and honey flow.
And we shall enjoy then
what he once did promise our fathers.
Almighty, thou art stronger
than Egyptian gods are.

153

*Pharao und seine Knechte schlägst du
  nieder.*
Von der Fron befrein uns Moses und Aron.

Ewiger Gott, wir dienen dir;
weihn dir unsere Opfer
und unsre Liebe:
Du hast uns auserwählt,
führst uns ins gelobte Land.
Wir werden frei sein!

(Ende des ersten Aktes.)

ZWISCHENSPIEL

CHOR
  Wo ist Moses?
  (geflüstert)
  Wo ist der Führer?
  Wo ist er?
  Lange schon hat ihn keiner gesehn!
  Nie kehrt er wieder!
  Verlassen sind wir!
  Wo ist sein Gott?
  Wo ist der Ewige?
  Wo ist Moses?

Thou wilt strike down Pharaoh and all
  his servants.
Now we're freed from toil by Moses and Aaron.
Infinite God, we worship thee,
consecrate to thee off'rings
and our devotion;
for thou hast chosen us,
lead'st us to the promised land.
We shall be free, free!

(*End of Act One.*)

INTERLUDE

CHORUS
  Where is Moses?
  (*whispered*)
  Where is our leader?
  Where is he?
  It's been a long time since he was seen!
  Ne'er shall we see him!
  Abandoned are we!
  Where is his god?
  Where is the infinite?
  Where is Moses?

II. AKT

1. SZENE: ARON UND DIE SIEBZIG ÄLTESTEN VOR DEM BERG DER OFFENBARUNG

DIE 70 ÄLTESTEN
Vierzig Tage!

PRIESTER
Vierzig Tage liegen wir nun schon hier!

70 ÄLTESTE
Wie lange noch?

PRIESTER
Wie lange soll das noch dauern?
Vierzig Tage warten wir nun auf Moses,
und noch immer weiß keiner Recht und Gesetz!
Unvorstellbares Gesetz des unvorstellbaren
Gottes!

EIN ÄLTESTER
Immer besetzt Juda die besten Weideplätze!

ZWEITER ÄLTESTER
Ärger als Ägypten,
zu Fron ohne Ruhetag
zwingt Ephraim Benjamins Söhne!

DRITTER ÄLTESTER
Benjamins Söhne haben Ephraims Weiber
geraubt!

156

ACT II

SCENE 1: AARON AND THE SEVENTY ELDERS BEFORE THE MOUNTAIN OF REVELATION

THE SEVENTY ELDERS
> Forty days now!

PRIEST
> Forty days now, yet we're still waiting here!

SEVENTY ELDERS
> When will this end?

PRIEST
> How long is this to continue?
> Forty days now we have awaited Moses,
> and still no one knows either law or command!
> Unperceivable command from one who's yet
> unperceived.

AN ELDER
> All of the best pastures are occupied by Judah!

ANOTHER ELDER
> Far worse than in Egypt,
> to toil without day of rest,
> as Ephraim makes Benjamin's sons do!

A THIRD ELDER
> Ephraim's women have been stolen by
> Benjamin's sons!

70 ÄLTESTE

Gewalt regiert!
Unzucht kennt ihre Strafe nicht,
Tugend nicht ihren Lohn!
Vierzig Tage warten wir vergebens
vor dieser Höhe!

ARON

Wenn Moses von dieser Höhe hernieder
steigt,
wo ihm allein das Gesetz sich offenbart,
soll mein Mund euch Recht und Gesetz
vermitteln.
Erwartet die Form nicht vor dem Gedanken!
Aber gleichzeitig wird sie da sein!

70 ÄLTESTE

Das wird zu spät kommen!
Das Volk ist verzweifelt!
Es mißtraut dieser Höhe,
deren Umzäunung es vom Berg der Offen-
barung trennt.
Es rast, es glaubt uns keinem mehr;
hält die Umzäunung für Willkür,
die Offenbarung für Ausflucht,
Moses' Schweigen für Flucht!

(Lärm aus weiter Ferne.)

Hört! Hört! Zu spät!

(Lärm, Geheule und Tosen kommt, immer
lauter, rasch näher: in wütender Erregung
stürzt von allen Seiten die brüllende
Volksmenge auf die Bühne.)

SEVENTY ELDERS

Thus might now reigns!
Lewdness knows not its punishment;
virtue knows not reward!
Forty days now we have waited vainly
before this summit!

AARON

When Moses has left the summit, come down
    from there,
from where the laws are revealed to him alone,
you shall hear both law and command from
    my mouth.
You cannot expect form before idea,
for together they'll make their appearance.

SEVENTY ELDERS

That is too late for us!
The people are downcast!
They distrust this high summit,
for the enclosure keeps the revelation far
    from them.
They rage, they trust not one of us,
think the enclosure is senseless,
the revelation is pretext,
Moses' silence means flight!

(*Noise in the far distance.*)

Hear! Hear! Too late!

(*Growing sounds of shouting and raging approach quickly; then in furious agitation the
roaring crowd rushes upon the stage from all
directions.*)

159

2. SZENE

CHOR

Wo ist Moses?
Daß wir ihn zerreißen!
Wo ist der Allgegenwärtige?
Daß er es mit ansieht!
Wo ist der Allmächtige?
Daß er uns daran hindre!
Fürchtet nichts! Zerreißt ihn!
Der Unvorstellbare hat es nicht verboten!
Gebt uns unsre Götter wieder,
daß sie Ordnung schaffen!
Oder wir zerreißen euch,
die ihr uns. Gesetz und Recht genommen habt!

70 ÄLTESTE

Aron, hilf uns! Sprich zu ihnen!
Sie morden uns! Dich hören sie!
Du hast ihr Herz!

ARON

Volk Israels!
Mein Bruder Moses weilt,
wo er immer ist,
ob er uns nah ist oder fern;
er weilt auf dieser Höhe:
bei seinem Gott.
Vielleicht hat er uns verlassen,
der uns fern war;
vielleicht hat sein Gott ihn verlassen,
dem er nah war;
vielleicht kam er ihm zu nah!
Es ist ein strenger Gott:
Vielleicht hat er ihn getötet!

SCENE 2

CHORUS
> Where is Moses?
> We'll tear him asunder!
> Where is the great omnipresent one?
> How can he condone this?
> Where is the almighty one?
> Why does he now impede us?
> Have no fear! Destroy him!
> The inconceivable god did not forbid it!
> Give us back our gods to worship;
> let them bring us order,
> lest we tear you limb from limb,
> you who took command and law away from us!

THE SEVENTY ELDERS
> Aaron, help us! Speak out for us!
> They'll murder us! They pay you heed!
> You have their hearts!

AARON
> O Israel,
> my brother Moses tarries
> where he always is,
> though he be near to us or far:
> he rests upon that summit,
> close to his god.
> It may be that he has left us,
> being far from us.
> Or maybe his god has now left him,
> being so near to him.
> Perhaps he approached too near!
> That god is so severe;
> it may be that he's destroyed him!

CHOR (eine Gruppe)
Sein Gott hat ihn getötet!

CHOR (andere Gruppe)
Die Götter haben ihn getötet!

CHOR (alle)
Die Götter haben ihn getötet!
Die starken Götter vernichten den Frevler!
Der Ew'ge konnt ihn nicht beschützen!
Der Unsichtbare kommt keinem zu Hilfe!
Der Unsichtbare läßt nirgends sich blicken!
Sein Gott ist machtlos!
Zerreißt sie, tötet seine Priester,
erschlagt sie, verbrennt sie,
die Priester dieses falschen Gottes!

70 ÄLTESTE
Aron, hilf uns; gib nach!

ARON
Volk Israels!
Deine Götter geb ich dir wieder
und dich ihnen;
wie es dich verlangt.
Lasset die Ferne dem Ewigen!
Euch gemäß sind Götter
gegenwärtigen, alltagsnahen Inhalts.
Ihr spendet diesen Stoff,
ich geb ihm solche Form:
Alltäglich, sichtbar, faßlich
in Gold verewigt.
Bringt Gold herbei!
Opfert! Ruft ihn an!
Ihr sollt glücklich werden!

CHORUS (*one group*)
>His god may have destroyed him!

CHORUS (*another group*)
>The gods have probably destroyed him!

CHORUS (*all*)
>The gods then have indeed destroyed him!
>The gods so mighty destroyed this offender!
>The infinite could not protect him!
>The great unseen one will never give us assistance!
>The great unseen one lets no one behold him!
>His god is powerless!
>O slay them, kill off all this priesthood.
>O smite them and burn them,
>the priesthood, servants of this false god!

SEVENTY ELDERS
>Aaron, help us. Relent!

AARON
>O Israel,
>I return your gods to you,
>and also give you to them,
>just as you have demanded.
>Leave distant things to one infinite,
>since to you the gods have
>ever-present and always-common substance.
>You shall provide the stuff;
>I shall give it a form:
>common and visible, imaged
>in gold forever.
>Bring out your gold!
>Yield it! Call him forth!
>You then shall be happy!

163

CHOR

Jubelt, freut euch! Juble, Israel!
Götter, Bilder unsres Auges,
Götter, Herren unsrer Sinne!
Ihre leibliche Sichtbarkeit,
Gegenwart, verbürgt unsre Sicherheit;
ihre Grenzen und Meßbarkeit
fordern nicht, was unserm Gefühl versagt,
Götter, nahe unserm Fühlen,
Götter, die wir ganz begreifen:
Tugend lohne Glückseligkeit,
Übeltat bestrafe Gerechtigkeit;
zeigend unsrer Taten Folgen,
Götter, stellt sich eure Macht dar.
Juble, Israel, freue dich!
Farbig ist diese Gegenwart,
düster ist jene Ewigkeit;
Lebenslust scheut ihr Ende nicht,
furchtlos sucht sie es freiwillig;
Lust grenzt an Leben und an Tod,
steigert zu dem von jenem sich;
Drohung entzündet Lebensmut,
Standhaftigkeit und Tapferkeit.
Deinen Göttern als Inhalt
gabst du dein Innres,
dein Lebensgefühl.
Deiner Götter Aussehn
sichert dein Gold:
entäußre dich sein!
Mach dich arm, mach sie reich:
Sie werden dich nicht hungern lassen!
Juble, Israel!
Juble!

CHORUS

Joyous Israel! Joyous Israel!
Our gods, imaged in our vision;
our gods, masters of our senses!
You are earthly and visible,
manifest, assuring our certainty.
Your extent and your finitude
do not ask for that which our hearts deny.
O gods, near to all our feelings,
O gods, we can understand you.
Virtue's prize is great ecstasy;
acts of wrong are punished by righteousness.
Show us how our deeds are answered.
O gods, let us see your power.
Joyous Israel, jubilate Israel!
Bright is this present instant,
dismal that distant timelessness.
Pleasure shuns not its consequence,
fearlessly seeks it out willingly.
Joy borders life and also death,
heightened by each, from each partakes.
Danger inflames our love of life,
steadfastness too, and bravery.
You have given your gods
your innermost feelings
as content and form.
Now your god's great glory
fastens your gold.
Renounce all your wealth!
Give your gold; make them rich!
They will not let you ever hunger!
Joyous Israel!
Joyous!

3. SZENE: DAS GOLDENE KALB UND DER ALTAR

ARON

Dieses Bild bezeugt,
daß in allem, was ist, ein Gott lebt.
Unwandelbar, wie ein Prinzip,
ist der Stoff, das Gold,
das ihr geschenkt habt;
anschaulich wandelbar,
wie alles andre: Zweite,
ist die Gestalt, die ich ihm gegeben.
Verehrt euch selbst in diesem Sinnbild!

(Schon während Arons letzer Ansprache
sind von verschiedenen Seiten her Züge
beladener Kamele, Esel, Pferde sowie
Lastträger und Wagen auf die Bühne
gekommen. Sie bringen Opfer herein, Gold,
Getreide, Weinschläuche, Ölschläuche,
Vieh und dergleichen mehr. An vielen
Plätzen der Vorder- und Hinterbühne wird
abgeladen und aufgeschichtet. Züge mit
Vieh aller Arten gehen vorüber.
Gleichzeitig werden an vielen Stellen
Vorbereitungen zum Schlachten getroffen:
das Vieh wird geschmückt, bekränzt;
Schlächter mit großen Messern treten auf,
umtanzen das Vieh in wilden Sprüngen.)

(Es wird langsam Abend. Die Schlächter
schlachten nun das Vieh, werfen
Fleischstücke in die Menge, die sich darum
balgt. Einzelne Personen laufen mit blutigen
Fleischstücken herum und verzehren sie roh.

SCENE 3: THE GOLDEN CALF AND THE ALTAR

AARON

> This gold image attests
> that in all things that are, a god lives.
> Unchangeable, e'en as a law,
> is the stuff, the gold
> that you have given.
> (Seemingly changeable,
> as all else must be.) Much less
> matters the shape that I have provided.
> Revere yourselves in this gold symbol!

> (*During Aaron's last speech processions of
> laden camels, asses, horses, porters, and
> wagons enter the stage from different
> directions, bringing offerings of gold, grain,
> skins of wine and oil, animals, and the like.
> At many places in the foreground and back-
> ground these are unloaded and piled up.
> Herds of all manner of animals pass by.
> Simultaneously, preparations for slaughter
> are to be seen at many places. The animals
> are decorated and wreathed. Butchers with
> large knives enter and with wild leaps
> dance around the animals.*)

> (*Slowly it becomes evening. The butchers
> now slaughter the animals and throw pieces
> of meat to the crowd which fights over them.
> Some run about with bloody pieces of meat,
> devouring them raw.*)

Inzwischen werden große Kessel gebracht.
Brennmaterial wird aufgeschichtet. Die
Kessel werden aufgehängt. Am Altar werden
Brandopfer dargebracht.)

(Tanz der Schlächter.)

(Eine Kranke wird auf einer Bahre
hereingetragen. Die Menge vorn macht
Platz, die Kranke wird vor dem Goldenen
Kalb abgesetzt.)

EINE KRANKE
O Götterbild,
du strahlst, du wärmst, du heilst,
wie niemals die Sonne geheilt.
Den Finger leg ich bloß auf dich,
und schon bewegen sich die lahmen Glieder.

(Mit zunehmender Dunkelheit werden Feuer und
Fackeln entzündet, Wein und Öl ausgeschenkt.)

CHOR (Bettlerinnen und Bettler; ganz nahe
     dem Kalb)
Hier, o Götter, nehmt die letzten Lumpen,
die uns vor Sonnenglut und Wüstenstaub
     geschützt haben.
Und hier die letzten Bissen,
die wir uns für morgen erbettelt haben.

(Einige Greise, die sich mühsam
herangeschleppt haben, stehen nun vor dem
Goldenen Kalb.)

CHOR (Greise)
Die letzten Augenblicke,

*Meanwhile large pots are brought and fires
prepared. Burnt offerings are brought to
the altar.)*

(Dance of the Butchers.)

*(An Invalid Woman is brought in on a litter.
The crowd in front makes room, and the
Invalid Woman is placed before the
golden calf.)*

INVALID WOMAN
O godly form,
your rays give warmth, you heal,
as never the sun's rays have healed.
I merely placed my hand on you,
and even now the crippled limbs begin moving.

*(As darkness falls, fires and torches are
lit and wine and oil distributed.)*

CHORUS *(Male and Female Beggars, quite close
to the calf)*
Here, O great gods, take the only tatters
that have protected us from desert sand
and sun's blazing.
And here are the last of our morsels,
those which we have begged for
tomorrow's sustenance.

*(Several Elderly Persons, who have
laboriously dragged themselves along, stand
now before the golden calf.)*

CHORUS *(Old Men)*
The final living moments

die wir noch zu leben haben,
nehmt sie als Opfer.

70 ÄLTESTE
Sie haben sich getötet.

(Galopp wird hörbar; nähert sich rasch;
das Volk, aufgeregt, stiebt auseinander; die
Stammesfürsten und der Ephraimit reiten
in wildem Galopp bis vor das Kalb; springen
dort ab; Umstehende halten die Pferde.)

DER EPHRAIMIT
Frei unter eigenen Herren,
unterwirft sich ein Volk nur Göttern,
die kraftvoll herrschen.
Stammesfürsten, huldigt mit mir
diesem Abbild geregelter Kräfte!

DIE STAMMESFÜRSTEN
Im Namen aller von uns geführten Stämme,
Götter, seht uns vor euch auf den Knien,
die höhere Macht der höchsten unterworfen.

CHOR
Frei unter eigenen Herren!

(Der Jüngling hat sich einen Weg durch
die Menge gebahnt. Er ist zum Skelett
abgemagert, sieht fiebrig aus. Mit einer
langen Latte, die er mit beiden Händen hält,
schlägt er auf die Umstehenden ein und will
sie zwingen, vom Götzendienst abzulassen.)

JÜNGLING
Gedankenhoch waren wir erhöht,

that are still remaining to us
we give as off'ring.

SEVENTY ELDERS

They've slain themselves in off'rings.

(*Galloping is heard; it approaches
quickly. The people, excited, disperse.
The Tribal Leaders and the Ephraimite
gallop up wildly before the calf and spring
to the ground. Bystanders hold the horses.*)

EPHRAIMITE

Free, under lords of their choosing,
they'll be governed by only those gods
who rule with power.
Tribal leaders, swear now with me
to this image of governing power.

TRIBAL LEADERS

We speak for all of the tribes that name us leaders:
O gods, see how we kneel down before you.
We yield to a power that's higher, being highest!

CHORUS

Free under lords of our choosing!

(*The Youth has cleared a path through the
crowd. He is shrunken to a skeleton, appears
feverish. With a long rod held in both
hands he strikes out at the bystanders,
trying to force them to give up the idol
worship.*)

YOUTH

As high as thought were we once upraised,

gegenwartsfern, zukunftsnah!
Lebenstief sind wir erniedrigt.
Zertrümmert sei dies Abbild des Zeitlichen!
Rein sei der Ausblick zur Ewigkeit!

(Der Ephraimit, der hinter dem Jüngling
gestanden ist, ergreift ihn am Genick und
drückt ihn zu Boden.)

DER EPHRAIMIT
Hier blick nun zur Ewigkeit,
wenn dir Lebensnähe so wenig wert ist.

(Die Stammesfürsten erschlagen den
Jüngling, dann besteigen sie ihre Pferde,
mischen sich, einzeln und unregelmaßig,
unter das Volk und verschwinden,
abreitend, unauffällig.)

(In der Volksmenge herrscht nach den
vorigen Handlungen der Hingabe und der
Opfer eine Lust, sich gegenseitig zu
beschenken, vor. Frauen schenken
einander Schmuck, Tücher und dergleichen,
Männer Waffen, Geräte und dergleichen,
man bietet einander Speisen und Getränke,
bekränzt sich und andere mit Blumen;
einer hilft dem andern bei jeglicher
Tätigkeit u. a. m.)

(Überall wird nun Wein in Strömen
ausgeschenkt. Eine wilde Trunkenheit
bemächtigt sich aller. Man wirft die
schweren Steinkrüge umher, begießt sich
gegenseitig mit Wein und gerät in tolles

present afar, future at hand!
Deep as life are we degraded.
Annihilate this image of the temporal;
clear be the view of eternity!

(*The Ephraimite, who stands behind the
Youth, seizes him by the neck and presses
him to the ground.*)

EPHRAIMITE
Here, view now eternity,
since your present life has so little value.

(*The Tribal Leaders slay the Youth,
mount their horses, mingle with people
individually and in disorder, then
disappear, riding off unobtrusively.*)

(*After the foregoing acts of renunciation
and offering there now reigns a desire for
mutual giving. Women give each other
jewellery, fabrics, and the like, while men
give each other weapons, implements, etc.
They offer each other food and drink, set
wreaths upon themselves and others. Some
help others with tasks, etc.*)

(*Everywhere now wine is given out in
streams. A wild drunkenness overtakes
everyone. Heavy stone jars are thrown
about. The people shower wine and
implements upon each other during*)

Tanzen, wobei es auch hie und da zu
Zwistigkeiten und Prügeleien kommt.)

(Orgie der Trunkenheit und des Tanzes.)

70 ÄLTESTE

Selig ist das Volk,
und groß zeigt ein Wunder,
was Begeistrung, was Entzückung imstande:
unverwandelt keiner, jeder erhoben,
unergriffen keiner, jeder ergreifend.
Menschentugend, kraftvoll, wiedererweckte:
Ernst und Freude, Maß und Übermaß,
Frohsinn, Glück und Sehnsucht, Schwung und Ruhe.
Besinnung, Gier, Entsagung, Geiz,
Verschwendung und Habsucht,
alles Schöne, Gute, Häßliche, Schlechte,
Eigenlebens Zeugnis, wahrnehmbar, fühlbar.
Sinn schenkt Seele Sinn erst.
Seele ist Sinn.
Götter, die ihr Seele schenktet,
Sinne, Seele wahrzunehmen.
Götter, seid gepriesen!

(Vier nackte Jungfrauen—eine
davon das Mädchen—treten vor das Kalb.)

MÄDCHEN

Du goldener Gott,
wie Lust durchströmt mich dein Glanz!
Was glänzt nur, ist gut.
Unangreifbare Tugend des Golds,
unverlierbare Jungfräulichkeit,
belohnt als Vorbild und Abbild.

174

extravagant dancing, whereupon quarrelling
and fighting break out here and there.)

(*Orgy of Drunkenness and Dancing.*)

SEVENTY ELDERS

Happy is this folk,
and great is the wonder
and the rapture, and the joy they've created.
None is untransfigured; each is exalted.
None is unaffected; each is enraptured.
Powerful human virtues are reawakened:
grave and joyful; temperate, dissolute;
cheerful, pleased, and longing, active, resting.
Repression, lust, abstention, greed,
profusion, and envy.
All of beauty, goodness, ugliness, evil,
all that can be witnessed, manifest, sensate.
Sense first gives to spirit sense.
Spirit then is sense.
Those gods who have given you spirit,
sense and spirit to affect you,
let them be exalted!

(*Four Naked Virgins, one of them the Girl, step*
before the calf.)

THE GIRL

O golden of gods,
your glow streams through me with pleasure!
What gleams must be good.
Unassailable virtue of gold,
its viriginity cannot be lost,
repaid as model and image.

4. NACKTE JUNGFRAUEN

O goldener Gott,

o Priester goldener Götter,

das Blut jungfräulicher Unberührtheit,

gleich Goldes metallischer Kälte,

zur Frucht nicht erwärmt,

oh, Götter, entzückt eure Priester,

entzückt uns zu erster und letzter Lust,

erhitzt unser Blut,

daß es zischend am kalten Gold verrauche!

O rotes Gold!

(Die Priester stürzen auf die
Jungfrauen zu, umarmen und
küssen sie lange. Hinter jedes Paar
stellt sich ein Mädchen, das ein
langes Schlachtmesser und ein Gefäß
zum Auffangen des Blutes hält.)

70 ÄLTESTE

Blutopfer!

(Die Mädchen reichen den Priestern die
Messer. Die Priester fassen die
Jungfrauen an der Gurgel und stoßen
ihnen das Messer ins Herz; die Mädchen
fangen das Blut in den Gefäßen auf, die
Priester gießen es auf den Altar.)

(Die Menge beginnt nun mit Verwüstung
und Selbstmord; es werden Geräte
zerschlagen, die Steinkrüge zerbrochen,
die Wagen zertrümmert, u. s. w. Man
schleudert alles mögliche umher: Schwerter,
Dolche, Beile, Lanzen, Krüge, Geräte, u. s. w.
Im Taumel werfen sich einzelne den

FOUR NAKED VIRGINS
O golden of gods,
O priests who serve gods so golden,
our blood, virginal and still unblemished,
is coldly metallic as gold is,
not warmed to bear fruit.
O great ones, enrapture your priesthood,
transport us, arouse us to first and last rapture.
Enkindle our blood,
let it hiss 'gainst cold gold as forth it rushes!
O crimson gold!

(The priests embrace and kiss the maidens.
Behind each pair a girl stands holding a
long butcher's knife and a jug for
catching the blood.)

SEVENTY ELDERS
Blood off'ring!

(The girls hand the priests the knives.
The priests seize the virgins' throats and
thrust the knives into their hearts. The
girls catch the blood in receptacles. The
priests pour it forth on the altar.)

(Destruction and suicide now begin
amongst the crowd. Implements are
shattered, stone jars are smashed, carts
destroyed, etc. Everything possible is flung
about: swords, daggers, axes, lances, jars,
implements, etc. In a frenzy some throw
themselves upon implements, weapons,

Gegenständen, Waffen und dergleichen
entgegen, andere stürzen sich in Schwerter,
wieder andere springen ins Feuer, laufen
brennend über die Bühne; einige springen
von hohen Felsen herab und dergleichen
mehr; hierzu wilde Tänze.)

(Erotische Orgie.)

(Ein nackter Jüngling läuft nach vorn, auf
ein Madchen zu, reißt ihm die Kleider vom
Leib, hebt es hoch und rennt mit ihm zum Altar.)

DER NACKTE JÜNGLING
Eurem Vorbild, Götter,
leben wir die Liebe nach!

(Viele Männer folgen diesem Beispiel, werfen
ihre Kleider ab, entkleiden Frauen und
tragen sie denselben Weg, am Altar
haltmachend, nach dem Hintergrund.)

EINIGE ANDERE NACKTE
Heilig ist die Zeugungskraft!

NOCH ANDERE
Heilig ist die Fruchtbarkeit!

VIELE ANDERE
Heilig ist die Lust!

(Ein ganzer Zug Nackter läuft auf diese
Weise mit Geschrei und Gejohle am Altar
vorbei und verschwindet im Hintergrund.
Die Bühne ist durch den Abzug der
Nackten leerer geworden; nun legt sich bald

and the like, while others fall upon swords.
Still others leap into the fire and run
burning across the stage. Several jump
down from the high rock, etc. Wild
dancing with all this.)

(Erotic Orgy.)

(A naked youth runs forward to a girl,
tears the clothes from her body, lifts her
high and runs with her to the altar.)

THE NAKED YOUTH
In your godly image
we shall let our passions live.

(Many men follow this example, throw
their clothes aside, strip women and bear
them off the same way, towards the
background, pausing at the altar.)

SEVERAL OTHER NAKED MEN
Holy is the creative power!

STILL OTHERS
Holy is fertility!

MANY OTHERS
Holy is desire!

(A whole succession of naked people,
screaming and yelling, run past the altar
in this manner and disappear in the background.
With the departure of the naked people
the stage has become emptier. The

179

alle Erregtheit; Taumel und Trunkenheit
gehen in Erschlaffung und Müdigkeit
über; viele sinken schlafend um oder
ziehen sich still zurück.
Aus dem Hintergrund klingt noch Musik
und Gesang, von immer anderen Stellen her.)

CHOR

Götter, die ihr Seele schenktet . . .
Sinne, Seele wahrzunehmen . . .
Du goldener Gott!
Gold glänzt wie Lust!
Menschentugend gleicht Gold!
Gold gleicht Lust!
Lust ist Wildheit!
Gold glänzt wie Blut!
Gold ist Herrschaft!
Hingabe!
Gerechtigkeit!
Verwirrender Glanz!

(Die Feuer erlöschen, bis auf wenige,
allmählich. Alle Bewegung auf der Bühne
hat aufgehört.)

4. SZENE

(In Hintergrund, möglichst weit hinten,
auf einem der Hügel, erhebt sich ein Mann,
blickt eine Weile in die Richtung, wo man
den Berg der Offenbarung zu denken hat,
weckt gestikulierend einige ihm zunächst
Liegende, die er veranlaßt, in dieselbe
Richtung zu blicken und ruft dann:)

excitement, frenzy, and drunkenness now
quickly pass into exhaustion and lassitude.
Many sink down, falling asleep.
Others withdraw quietly.
From the background come music and
singing, always from different places.)

CHORUS

Great gods who have given you spirit . . .
Senses, spirit to affect you . . .
O golden of gods.
Gold gleams like lust!
Human virtue is gold-like!
Gold is lust!
Lust is wildness!
Gold gleams like blood!
Gold is power,
devotion,
and righteousness!
Bewildering gleam!

(The fires die out gradually, until only a
few remain. All motion on the stage
has ceased.)

SCENE 4

(In the background, as far back as possible, a
man on one of the hillocks raises himself
up, peers for a time in the direction where
the mountain of revelation is supposed to
be, then, gesticulating, he awakens several
of those lying near him and has them look
in the same direction. He cries out:)

EIN MANN

Moses steigt vom Berg herab!

(Auf diesen Ruf hin erwachen allenthalben
die Schlafenden, erheben sich, und von
allen Seiten strömt wieder Volk herbei.)

MOSES

Vergeh, du Abbild des Unvermögens,
das Grenzelose in ein Bild zu fessen!

(Das Goldene Kalb vergeht; das Volk
weicht zurück und verschwindet rasch von
der Bühne.)

CHOR

Der Strahl des Goldes erlischt;
Unser Gott ist wieder unsichtbar.
Alle Lust, alle Freude, alle Hoffnung ist weg!
Alles wieder trüb und lichtlos!
Laßt uns den Gewaltigen fliehn!

(Alle ab bis auf Moses und Aron.)

5. SZENE: MOSES UND ARON

MOSES

Aron, was hast du getan?

ARON

Nichts Neues!
Nur, was stets meine Aufgabe war:
Wenn dein Gedanke kein Wort,
mein Wort kein Bild ergab,

MAN

Moses is descending from the mountain!

(*After this cry, those sleeping awaken
everywhere, arise, and from all sides
people again stream in.*)

MOSES

Begone, you image of powerlessness
to enclose the boundless in an image finite!

(*The golden calf vanishes. The crowd
moves back and quickly disappears from
the stage.*)

CHORUS

The golden rays are now quenched!
Once again our god cannot be seen.
Every joy, every pleasure, every promise is gone!
All is once more gloom and darkness!
We must now escape from his might!

(*Exit all but Moses and Aaron.*)

SCENE 5: MOSES AND AARON

_____

MOSES

Aaron, O what have you done?

AARON

Naught diff'rent,
just my task as it ever has been:
When your idea gave forth
no word, my word gave forth

183

vor ihren Ohren, ihren Augen ein,
Wunder zu tun.

MOSES

Auf wessen Geheiß?

ARON

Wie immer:
ich hörte die Stimme in mir.

MOSES

Ich habe nicht gesprochen.

ARON

Aber ich habe dennoch verstanden.

MOSES

Schweig!

ARON

Dein . . . Mund . . .
Du warst lange fern von uns . . .

MOSES

Bei meinem Gedanken!
Das müßte dir nahe sein!

ARON

Wenn du dich einsam machst,
wirst du tot geglaubt.
Das Volk hat auf das Wort deines Mundes,
dem Recht und Gesetz entspringen,
lange gewartet.
So mußte ich ihm ein Bild zu schauen geben.

MOSES

Dein Bild verblich vor meinem Wort!

184

no image for them, I worked marvels
for eyes and ears to witness.

MOSES

Commanded by whom?

AARON

As always,
I heeded the voice from within.

MOSES

But I did not instruct you.

AARON

Nevertheless, I still comprehended.

MOSES

Cease!

AARON

Your . . . mouth . . .
You were far away from us . . .

MOSES

There with my idea.
That must have been close to you.

AARON

When you remained apart
we believed you were dead.
And since the people had long expected
both law and commandment soon
to issue from your mouth,
I was compelled to provide an image for them.

MOSES

Your image faded at my word!

185

ARON

Deinem Wort waren sonst Bilder
und Wunder, die du mißachtest, versagt.
Und doch war das Wunder nicht mehr als ein Bild:
als dein Wort mein Bild zerstörte.

MOSES

Gottes Ewigkeit vernichtet Göttergegenwart!
Das ist kein Bild, kein Wunder!
Das ist das Gesetz.
Das Unvergängliche, sag es,
wie diese Tafeln, vergänglich;
in der Sprache deines Mundes!

(Er hält Aron die Tafeln hin.)

ARON

Israels Bestehn bezeuge den Gedanken
des Ewigen!

MOSES

Ahnst du nun die Allmacht des
Gedankens über die Worte und Bilder?

ARON

Ich verstehe es so:
dieses Volk soll erhalten bleiben.
Aber ein Volk kann nur fühlen.
Ich liebe dieses Volk,
ich lebe für es
und will es erhalten!

MOSES

Um des Gedankens willen!
Ich liebe meinen Gedanken und lebe für ihn!

AARON

> But your word was denied image
> and marvel, which are detested by you.
> And yet was the marvel an image, not more,
> when your word destroyed my image.

MOSES

> God's eternity opposes idols' transience!
> No image this, no marvel!
> These are the commands!
> The everlasting one spoke them,
> just as these tables so temp'ral,
> in the language you are speaking.

> (*He holds out the tables to Aaron.*)

AARON

> Israel endures, thus proving the idea
> of one timeless.

MOSES

> Grant you now the power which
> idea has over both word and image?

AARON

> I discern only this:
> that this folk shall remain protected.
> And yet, they've naught but their feeling.
> I love this humble folk.
> I live just for them
> and want to sustain them.

MOSES

> If the idea wills it.
> My love is for my idea. I live just for it!

ARON

> *Auch du würdest dies Volk lieben,*
> *hättest du gesehn, wie es lebt,*
> *wenn es sehen, fühlen, hoffen darf.*
> *Kein Volk kann glauben, was es nicht fühlt.*

MOSES

> *Du erschütterst mich nicht!*
> *Es muß den Gedanken erfassen!*
> *Es lebt nur deshalb!*

ARON

> *Ein beklagenswertes, ein Volk von*
> *Märtyrern wäre es dann!*
> *Kein Volk erfaßt mehr als einen Teil*
> *des Bildes, das den faßbaren Teil des*
> *Gedankens ausdrückt.*
> *So mache dich dem Volk verständlich,*
> *auf ihm angemeßne Art.*

MOSES

> *Ich soll den Gedanken verfälschen?*

ARON

> *Laß mich ihn auflösen!*
> *Umschreibend, ohne auszusprechen:*
> > *Verbote,*
> *furchterregend, doch befolgbar,*
> *sichern das Bestehen;*
> *die Notwendigkeit verklärend:*
> > *Gebote, hart,*
> *doch hoffnungserweckend,*
> *verankern den Gedanken.*
> *Unbewußt wird getan, wie du willst.*
> *Menschlich schwankend wirst du dein Volk*
> > *dann finden,*
> *doch liebenswert!*

AARON

> You also would have loved this people,
> had you only seen how they lived
> when they dared to see and feel and hope.
> No folk is faithful, unless it feels.

MOSES

> You have shaken me not!
> They must comprehend the idea!
> They live for that end!

AARON

> What a piteous people, a folk made of
> martyrs they would then be!
> No folk can grasp more than just a
> partial image, the perceivable part
> of the whole idea.
> Be understood by all the people
> in their own accustomed way.

MOSES

> Am I to debase the idea?

AARON

> Let me present it then,
> describing without specifying:
>> Restrictions,
> fear-inspiring yet not too harsh,
> further perseverance;
> the need thus will be the clearer.
>> Commandments stern
> give rise to new hoping
> and strengthen the idea.
> Unbeknown, what you want will be done.
> Human wavering you'll find your people
>> still have . . .
> yet worthy of love.

MOSES

Das will ich nicht erleben!

ARON

Du mußt leben!
Du kannst nicht anders!
Du bist an deinen Gedanken gebunden!

MOSES

Ja, an meinen Gedanken, wie ihn diese
Tafeln ausdrücken . . .

ARON

. . . die auch nur ein Bild,
ein Teil des Gedankens sind.

MOSES

So zertrümmere ich diese Tafeln und
will Gott bitten, daß er mich von
diesem Amt abberuft.

(Er zertrümmert die Tafeln.)

ARON

Kleinmütiger!
Du, der du Gottes Wort hast,
ob mit, ob ohne Tafeln:
Ich, dein Mund, bewahre deinen Gedanken,
wie immer ich ihn ausspreche.

MOSES

Durch Bilder!

ARON

Bilder deines Gedankens:
sie sind er, wie alles, was aus ihm hervorgeht.

190

MOSES

I shall not live to see it!

AARON

Go on living!
Aught else is futile!
You're bounden to your idea so closely!

MOSES

Bounden to my idea, as e'en do these
tables set it forth.

AARON

They're images also,
just part of the whole idea.

MOSES

Then I smash to pieces both these tables,
and I shall also ask him to
withdraw the task given me.

(*He smashes the tables.*)

AARON

Faint-hearted one!
You, who yet have God's message,
without or with the tables.
I, your mouth, do rightly guard your idea
whenever I do utter it.

MOSES

In image!

AARON

Image of your idea;
they are one, as all is that emerges from it.

Ich beuge mich der Notwendigkeit;
denn dieses Volk soll erhalten bleiben,
um für den Ewigkeitsgedanken zu zeugen.
Meine Bestimmung, es schlechter zu sagen,
als ich es verstehe.
Wissende jedoch werden ihn
immer wiederfinden!

CHOR (zieht im Hintergrund vorüber, geführt von
    einer Feuersäule.)
Er hat uns auserwählt vor allen Völkern,
das Volk des einz'gen Gotts zu sein;
ihm allein zu dienen,
keines andern Knecht!

ARON
Sieh hin!

MOSES
Die Feuersäule!

ARON
Sie führt uns bei Nacht—
Der Allmächtige gibt durch mich dem
Volk ein Zeichen.

(Es wird im Hintergrund rasch Tag, die
Feuersäule verblaßt und verwandelt sich in
die Wolkensäule. Der Vordergrund bleibt
verhältnismäßig finster.)

MOSES
Die Wolkensäule!

ARON
Sie führt uns bei Tag.

I simply yield before necessity;
for it is certain this folk will be sustained
to give proof of the eternal idea.
This is my mission: to speak it more simply
than I understand it.
Yet, the knowing ones surely will
ever again discover it!

CHORUS (*moving past in the background, led by a pillar
   of fire.*)
For he has chosen us before all others
as his folk, to serve the only God,
him alone to worship,
serving no one else!

AARON
   Look there!

MOSES
   The fiery pillar!

AARON
   To lead us by night—
   Thus through me has God given a signal
   to the people.

   (*In the background day arrives quickly. The
   pillar of fire fades and is transformed into
   the pillar of cloud. The foreground remains
   relatively dark.*)

MOSES
   The cloudlike pillar!

AARON
   It leads us by day.

MOSES

Götzenbilder!

ARON

Gottes Zeichen, wie der glühende Dornbusch
Darin zeigt der Ewige nicht sich,
aber den Weg zu sich;
und den Weg ins gelobte Land!

CHOR

Er wird uns führen in das Land,
wo Milch und Honig fließt,
und wir sollen genießen,
was er unsern Vätern verheißen.

(Aron langsam ab in den Hintergrund.)

CHOR

Allmächt'ger,
du bist stärker als Ägyptens
Götter!

MOSES

Unvorstellbarer Gott!
Unaussprechlicher, vieldeutiger Gedanke!
Läßt du diese Auslegung zu?
Darf Aron, mein Mund, dieses Bild machen?
So habe ich mir ein Bild gemacht, falsch,
wie ein Bild nur sein kann!
So bin ich geschlagen!
So war alles Wahnsinn, was ich
gedacht habe,
und kann und darf nicht gesagt werden
O Wort, du Wort, das mir fehlt!

(Moses sinkt verzweifelt zu Boden.)

194

MOSES

> Godless image!

AARON

> God-sent signal, burning bush again glowing.
> The infinite thus shows not himself,
> but shows the way to him
> and the way to the promised land!

CHORUS

> He will then lead us to the land
> where milk and honey flow,
> and we shall enjoy then
> what he once did promise our fathers.

(*Aaron slowly exits in the background.*)

CHORUS

> Almighty,
> thou art stronger than Egyptian
> gods are!

MOSES

> Inconceivable God!
> Inexpressible, many-sided idea,
> will you let it be so explained?
> Shall Aaron, my mouth, fashion this image?
> Then I have fashioned an image too, false,
> as an image must be.
> Thus am I defeated!
> Thus, all was but madness that
> I believed before,
> and can and must not be given voice.
> O word, thou word, that I lack!

(*Moses sinks to the ground in despair.*)

(*End of Act Two.*)

III. AKT

1. SZENE

(Moses tritt auf; ihm folgt Aron,
ein Gefangener in Fesseln. Er wird
hereingeschleift von zwei Kriegern, an
Schultern und Armen festgehalten.
Nach ihm die 70 Ältesten.)

MOSES
Aron, nun ist es genug!

ARON
Willst du mich morden?

MOSES
Es geht nicht um dein Leben . . .

ARON
Das gelobte Land . . .

MOSES
Ein Bild . . .

ARON
In Bildern sollte ich reden,
wo du in Begriffen;
zum Herzen,
wo du zum Hirn sprichst—

MOSES
Du, dem das Wort mit dem Bild davonläuft,

ACT III

SCENE 1

(Moses enters. Aaron, a prisoner in chains, follows, dragged in by two soldiers who hold him fast by the shoulders and arms. Behind him come the Seventy Elders.)

MOSES
Aaron, now this must cease!

AARON
Will you then kill me?

MOSES
It is not a matter of your life . . .

AARON
The promised land . . .

MOSES
An image . . .

AARON
I was to speak in images
while you spoke in ideas;
I was to speak to the heart,
you to the mind.

MOSES
You, from whom both word and image flee,

197

du weilst selbst, lebst selbst
in den Bildern, die du vorgibst,
fürs Volk zu erzeugen.

Dem Ursprung, dem Gedanken entfremdet,

genügt dir dann weder das Wort noch das Bild . . .

ARON (unterbrechend)
. . . sichtbare Wunder sollte ich tun,
wo das Wort und das Bild des Mundes
versagten . . . !

MOSES
. . . da genügte dir nur mehr die Tat,
die Handlung?
Da machtest du den Stab zum Führer,
meine Kraft zum Befreier,
und Nilwasser beglaubigte die Allmacht . . .

Da begehrtest du leiblich, wirklich,
mit Füßen zu betreten ein unwirkliches Land,
wo Milch und Honig fließt.
Da schlugst du auf den Felsen,
statt zu ihm zu sprechen, wie dir befohlen,

daß Wasser aus ihm fließe . . .
Aus dem nackten Felsen sollte das Wort

Erquickung schlagen . . .

ARON
Niemals kam dein Wort ungedeutet
ans Volk.
Mit dem Stab deshalb sprach ich zum Felsen
in seiner Sprache, die auch das Volk versteht.

you yourself remain, you yourself live
in the images that you have provided
for the people to witness.
Having been alienated from the source,
     from the idea,
then neither word nor image satisfied you . . .

AARON (*interrupting*)
     I was to perform visible marvels
     when the word and the image from
          the mouth failed . . . !

MOSES
     . . . but you were satisfied only by the act,
          the deed.
     You then made of the rod a leader,
     of my power a liberator.
     And the waters of the Nile attested the
          supreme might . . .
     You then desired actually, physically,
     to tread with your feet upon an unreal land
     where milk and honey flowed.
     You then struck the rock,
     instead of speaking to it, as you were
          commanded to do
     in order to make water flow forth from it . . .
     The word alone was to have struck forth
          refreshment
     from the naked rock . . .

AARON
     Never did your word reach the people
          without meaning.
     And thus did I speak to the rock
     in its language, which the people also understand.

MOSES

Du sagst es schlechter, als du es verstehst,
denn du weißt, daß der Felsen ein Bild,
wie die Wüste und der Dornbusch:
drei, die dem Leib nicht geben,
was er braucht gegen den Geist,
der Seele, was deren Wunschlosigkeit
zu ewigem Leben genug ist.

Auch der Felsen, wie alle Bilder,
gehorcht dem Wort,
daraufhin er Erscheinung geworden war.
So gewannst du das Volk nicht für den Ewigen,
sondern für dich . . .

ARON

Für seine Freiheit,
daß es ein Volk werde!

MOSES

Dienen, dem Gottesgedanken zu dienen,
ist die Freiheit, zu der
dieses Volk auserwählt ist.
Du aber unterwarfst es fremden Göttern,
unterwarfst es dem Kalb und der
Feuer- und der Wolkensäule.
Denn du tust wie das Volk,
weil du fühlst wie es und so denkst.
Und der Gott, den du zeigst,
ist ein Bild der Ohnmacht,
ist abhängig von einem Gesetz über sich;
muß erfüllen, was er versprochen hat;
muß tun, um was er gebeten wird,
ist gebunden an sein Wort.
Wie die Menschen handeln—gut
oder böse—so muß er:

MOSES

> You speak more simply than you understand,
> for you know that the rock is, like the
> wasteland and the burning bush—
> three that give not to the body
> what it needs with regard to spirit—
> is, I say, an image of the soul,
> whose very renunciation is sufficient for
>   eternal life.
> And the rock, even as all images,
> obeys the word,
> from whence it came to be manifested.
> Thus, you won the people not for the eternal one,
> but for yourself . . .

AARON

> For their freedom—
> so that they would become a nation.

MOSES

> To serve, to serve the divine idea
> is the purpose of the freedom for which
> this folk has been chosen.
> You, however, expose them to strange gods,
> to the calf
> and to the pillars of fire and cloud;
> for you do as the people do,
> because you feel and think as they do.
> And the god that you showed to them
> is an image of powerlessness,
> is dependent upon a power beyond itself,
> must fulfil what it has promised,
> must do what it is asked,
> is bound by its word.
> Just as men act—well
> or badly—so must it;

strafen ihr Böses, belohnen ihr Gutes.

Aber der Mensch ist unabhängig und tut,
was ihm beliebt aus freiem Willen.
Hier beherrschen die Bilder bereits
den Gedanken, statt ihn auszudrücken.
Ein Allmächtiger—was immer er auch halte

—ist zu nichts verpflichtet,
durch nichts gebunden.
Ihn bindet nicht die Tat des Frevlers,
nicht das Gebet des Guten,
nicht das Opfer des Reuigen.
Bilder führen und beherrschen dieses Volk,
das du befreit hast:
und fremde Wünsche sind seine Götter
und führen es zurück in die Sklaverei
der Gottlosigkeit und der Genüsse.
Verraten hast du Gott an die Götter,
den Gedanken an die Bilder,
dieses auserwählte Volk an die andern,
das Außergewöhnliche an die Gewöhnlichkeit . . .

DIE KRIEGER
Sollen wir ihn töten?

MOSES (an alle)
Immer, wenn ihr euch unter die Völker mischt
und verwendet euere Gaben,
die zu besitzen ihr auserwählt seid,
um für den Gottesgedanken zu kämpfen,
und ihr verwendet euere Gaben zu falschen
und nichtigen Zwecken, um im Wettbewerb
mit fremden Völkern an ihren Niedrigen
    Freuden teilzunehmen,
immer, wenn ihr die Wunschlosigkeit

it must punish their wickedness, reward
  their virtues.
But man is independent and does
what pleases him, according to free will.
Here images govern
the idea, instead of expressing it.
The almighty one (and he retains that
  quality forever)
is not obliged to do anything,
is bound by nothing.
He is bound neither by the transgressor's deeds,
nor by the prayers of the good,
nor by the offerings of the penitent.
Images lead and rule this folk
that you have freed,
and strange wishes are their gods,
leading them back to the slavery
of godlessness and earthly pleasures.
You have betrayed God to the gods,
the idea to images,
this chosen folk to others,
the extraordinary to the commonplace . . .

SOLDIERS
  Shall we kill him?

MOSES (*addressing all*)
  Whensoever you went forth amongst the people
  and employed those gifts—
  which you were chosen to possess
  so that you could fight for the divine idea—
  whensoever you employed those gifts for false
  and negative ends, that you might
  rival and share the lowly pleasures of strange
    peoples,
  and whensoever you had abandoned

der Wüste verlaßt
und euere Gaben euch zur höchsten Höhe
    geführt haben,
immer werdet ihr wieder
heruntergestürzt werden vom Erfolg des
Mißbrauches, zurück in die Wüste.

(Zu den Kriegern)
Gebt ihn frei, und wenn er es vermag,
so lebe er.

(Aron frei, steht auf und fällt tot um.)

MOSES
    Aber in der Wüste seid ihr unüberwindlich
    und werdet das Ziel erreichen:
        Vereinigt mit Gott.

Ende der Oper

the wasteland's renunciation
and your gifts had led you to the highest
    summit,
then as a result of that misuse
you were and ever shall be hurled back
into the wasteland.

(*To the Soldiers*)
Set him free, and if he can,
he shall live.

(*Aaron, free, stands up and then falls down dead.*)

MOSES
    But in the wasteland you shall be
    invincible and shall achieve the goal:
        unity with God.

The End

Index